When Life Hits the Fan

A Mindful Guide to Caring for Yourself While Caring for Others

Janet Fouts

When Life Hits the Fan – A Mindful Guide to Caring for Yourself While Caring for Others © 2018 by Janet Fouts. All rights reserved.

No part of this book may be reproduced or transmitted in any form or by any means without written permission from the author.

For information email janet@janetfouts.com

Author's note: The advice in this book is general and not meant to replace formal medical, psychological, or other treatment. If in need of expert assistance, consult with your therapist or doctor as relevant to your own care.

ISBN 978-0-69-216033-6

I dedicate this to CJ. My great love, my confidant, my best friend, and my anchor. Thank you for your smile, your love, encouragement, and trust.

Acknowledgements

I am humbled and grateful for all of you who shared your stories, your tears, your challenges, and your hearts for this book. I have learned so much from you. Together we are stronger! Thank you from the bottom of my heart.

When it dawned on me how important this book was to me and what a jumbled mess of information I wanted to share, I knew I needed help. Many thanks to Timothy Pratt, who edited and coached me through the process of making the book better with a kind and wise heart and who prodded in all the right ways.

Table of Contents

Acknowledgements 4

Foreword 1

Introduction. 3

Chapter 1:
How Did I Get Here? 7

Chapter 2:
The Caregiver Crisis 25

Chapter 3:
You Are Not Prepared For This 33

Chapter 4:
What Stress Does to Our Heads and Bodies . . . 47

Chapter 5:
The Role of Compassion. 65

Chapter 6:
You Can Build Resilience. 83

Chapter 7:
Allowing Others to Help. 101

Chapter 8:
Put Mindful Awareness to Work for You. 121

Index 143

About the Author 146

Journal 148

Foreword

I have long taught and believed in self-compassion first. Without care and love for one's self, there can be no real compassion for others. But this is a hard thing to remember when you're in the midst of caring for someone else around the clock.

Who cares for the caregiver? Often this strength has to come from within. We have to find self-compassion before we can be compassionate towards anyone else, but that's a tough ask when we are in the midst of caring for a loved one with tremendous need. It's an even tougher ask to remind ourselves to stand back and give ourselves breathing space every once in a while.

I have been in the role of caregiver for a dying parent and for my children when they have been ill. I know how it is to feel exhausted and tired at the end of a long day. As part of my own coping mechanisms, I use mindfulness and compassion, often on the spot as well as on the cushion, and they are a tremendous support in trying times. Many of my students have also found them invaluable when they are in personal or professional caregiving roles. People have been using these very practices for centuries to support their resilience in the face of hardship.

Yet, these concepts are often foreign to those that tend to need them the most. This is precisely what Janet does beautifully by making mindfulness and compassion for the caregiver accessible and practical.

In this book, Janet does a beautiful job of using poignant stories about caregivers in diverse contexts, all suffering from caretaker burnout. She weaves in her own story of burnout and suffering in order to bring readers clear and simple steps of ways to step back, be present, and take care of yourself so you can be resilient and effective in your care for others.

Personal, passionate, and truthful. This is the guide that every caretaker needs to read.

Leah Weiss, PhD, Author of: *HOW WE WORK: Live Your Purpose, Reclaim Your Sanity, and Embrace the Daily Grind*

Introduction

This book came to me after a particularly tough episode in my life, when caring for the love of my life, CJ, who is also a breast cancer patient.

These were dark, stressful times; times when I questioned everything I did, and fell into a deep depression.

I needed to find a better way to care for myself as well as CJ, and I dove back into some self-care practices I had used in the past, like meditation and Tai Chi. In order to take care of myself and stop the downward spiral I was in I had to take control of my life and embody my understanding of mindfulness practices.

In less time than I expected, I found an inner calm that helped me see a light at the end of the tunnel. I spoke to some friends who were going through their own challenges, and changing perspectives helped them too. I wanted to understand better what my fellow caregivers were going through and how I could help more people learn to manage the caregiving experience.

Because I live at least half my life on the internet, I started asking through my social media accounts to talk to people who were caregivers in some way. During the last year or so, I interviewed more than 50 everyday people who were caring for a loved one or family member. Those they cared for ranged from children to adults, with autism, bipolar disorder, disabilities, strokes, heart attacks, Crohn's disease, critical illnesses, Cancer, Parkinson's disease, dementia, Alzheimer's and some rare diseases I had never heard of.

As I went through my own experience, interviewed others, and dug into research, I discovered a way of being through mindfulness and emotional intelligence that gave me some ease in my life, happiness even. I took charge of my life again. And I saw what mindfulness was doing to help others in a variety of ways.

Even though I am actively involved in caregiving, I am able to use what I've learned to take better care of my love, myself and our family. Through this book and my website, I'll share what I have learned with others who are struggling with the weight and responsibility of taking care of loved ones.

Professional caregivers too will find these tools useful. They are under immense stress on a daily basis and also need to practice self-care. I hope that we can all find strength together.

If the term mindfulness brings up the vision of sitting in meditation and chanting, just file that image away. Suspend your preconceived notions of mindfulness and meditation, and trust me. You'll see.

Mindfulness is the practice of paying attention to what is here, right now. It's the paying attention that allows us to get past our set ideas of what should happen next. It allows us to more clearly understand ourselves and others. It allows us to find happiness and even joy in where we are right now, however grave our situation may be.

Another thing I'd like you to take away from this book is the knowledge that you are not alone. There are tools that can help you take care of your loved one and your own health too. Use the stories here as lessons. Use the tools and techniques provided to gain a little more hold on your life. Use what works for you. If meditation is something you are interested in, cool. There are guided meditations for you in the book and on the website that you'll find useful.

If meditation doesn't interest you? Not a problem, you don't have to meditate to be mindful. Nor do you need to be a Buddhist or any other religion. This is purely about paying attention, understanding yourself and others a bit more deeply, and being present in the moment when you need to be.

Chapter 1:

How Did I Get Here?

"When we protect ourselves so we won't feel pain, that protection becomes like armor, armor that imprisons the softness of the heart."
  —Pema Chödrön

About 12 years ago we had just moved into our first home together in San Jose, Ca, full of hope for our future.

A few months after we got settled in, my partner CJ was driving our son to preschool for his very first day, and something happened that foreshadowed how our lives were about to be turned upside down.

A car stopped right in front of her and she couldn't avoid hitting it. Little damage was done, no one was hurt, but the driver of the car she hit was visibly shaken and distraught. The woman seemed so upset for a minor fender-bender, and as CJ gently talked her down she found out why.

It turned out the woman had breast cancer, and was on her way to her third chemotherapy appointment. She told CJ how weak and sick chemo made her, that she was sometimes dizzy, and that her brain felt foggy at times. She apologized profusely and CJ did her best to comfort her, and waited for someone to come and drive with her to her appointment.

The incident left CJ a bit shaken and sorry for the woman and what she was going through. Fortunately, no one was hurt and CJ took our son to school, driving just a bit more carefully.

That same afternoon CJ got her own diagnosis. She'd gone to her doctor about a suspicious lump, and our worst fears were realized. She too had breast cancer. The tumor was large. Surgery and chemo would start immediately.

The diagnosis and treatment plan were so....clinical and devoid of compassion.

"You have breast cancer. I referred you to the surgeon who will do a mastectomy immediately. An Oncologist will meet with you and recommend you start chemotherapy as soon as it heals," said one doctor. "There will be a round of radiation afterwards and if it doesn't thicken your skin too much, we may be able to do reconstruction," said another.

All this was laid out like we were ordering blinds for the windows. No hint of humanity or concern for how she was taking it. As though this news would have no impact beyond a little surgery and some drug treatments. Oh, and radiation too. Let's not forget that.

Needless to say, we were shell-shocked.

Being two geeky types, we went home and immediately flew into research mode online.

What were our options? What did these drugs do and how did they work? How was all of this going to change our lives?

There was so much conflicting information about potential treatments, surgery and prognosis. Deep in the online forums the patients undergoing treatment told horror stories from their experiences. The sense of loss and fear was terrifying.

We found a flood of information to process. Some sources seemed reliable, backed by studies and data, and others seemed a bit more like snake oil vendors, preying on the desperation of the patient. We immediately learned that every cancer, and every single patient, responds differently to treatment.

And me? I found myself thrown into learning about the medical system, trying to decipher all of this, and becoming an advocate for the best possible care for the most important person in my life.

It didn't take long for us to have a lot of questions. chemotherapy (chemo) wreaks havoc on the body. The goal of chemo is to stop the rapid dividing of cancer cells, which is good, but it also affects healthy cells. That's why chemo patients often lose their hair, one of the most identifiable signs of a patient in chemo. Like cancer cells, hair cells are also rapidly dividing and so chemo destroys or delays their growth too.

Hair loss is just the beginning. There are a myriad of potential side effects to chemo, depending on what chemicals are used in treatment.

Side effects can include pain, swelling or weakness in the hands and feet, an array of digestive disruptions and nausea, extreme tiredness, "chemo fog" a form (just like the woman in the accident!), memory loss or disorientation, anxiety, stress, and anemia or low white cell counts in the blood. Several of these symptoms can disrupt treatment and put the patient at risk of infection.

Not everyone has any or all of these symptoms. Side effects may depend on other factors such as age or preexisting conditions. There are so many forms of chemo treatments to consider we can't lump them all in one bucket. Besides, most chemo involves a cocktail of drugs concocted to suit the particular cancer and patient.

I was in "fix-it mode" and then some. One of my favorite authors, Lynn Grabhorn, calls this mode "Heigh Ho Silvering" -- As though I could be the Lone Ranger and save the day!

After meeting the oncologist, we requested a meeting with a nutritionist to see how diet could help in the fight. The nutritionist told us the risk of a low white cell count ruled out fresh vegetables or fruit; everything had to be frozen or canned.

We'd need a strict dietary regimen during, and maybe after chemo. We asked about alternative medical options like naturopathy or herbal supplements to support her wellbeing -- and got a strong, NO WAY!

We were referred to a plastic surgeon to discuss reconstruction options. When we got to the waiting room, it was busy, with a long line of people waiting to register. When it was our turn the receptionist loudly asked, "Oh, you're here for breast reconstruction after a mastectomy, right? You'll need to watch this video before you see the doctor." She led us over to a kiosk on the side of the waiting room. In full view of everyone, we sat down to watch a movie which graphically broke down the options for reconstruction. One of these, "flap reconstruction," entails moving tissue from the belly, thigh, or back to replace the breast. There are several options, but to watch the movie and discuss them together in front of a whole roomful of patients was difficult and humiliating.

It got worse when we got in to see the doctor. We let him know that we felt a little more privacy was in order and began to ask the questions we'd written down after the video. He answered them while he examined her. Then he told us reconstruction would depend on the elasticity in her skin after the radiation. Radiation can make the skin thick and tough, like saddle leather, and then reconstruction is a challenging option. CJ burst into tears. The doctor responded by saying he didn't know why she was so upset. "It's only a breast, it's not like you are losing a leg or something," he added, and went on to describe how he had seen much more serious cases in his practice and suggested we just "go with it" and see what happened after radiation.

For the most part, we felt these doctors were just going through the motions, moving patients through a prescribed pattern, disengaged from the personal aspects of care.

CJ and I are a very tightly knit team. We did our research together and discussed in advance the questions for which we needed to get answers. The doctors weren't so excited to deal with questions from me. Each of them answered questions from CJ, as one would expect, but my questions went ignored unless she repeated them to the doctor herself. It was aggravating to both of us to feel like cogs in a machine, and I especially felt like an outsider who should just sit quietly and do as told.

Yeah...

So not me to sit obediently and wait quietly for the doctors to decide what happens next. And not my beloved partner either. We aren't the "sit still and do as you're told" types. Not at all.

From our research we thought the recommended approach outdated and too conservative. Frustrated, pissed off, and more than a little scared, we found a new oncologist.

He was kind and listened to our concerns. While his hospital didn't support homeopathy, he knew an oncologist in San Francisco who was more progressive in his treatment plan, and whom he trusted.

After consulting the oncologist at UCSF we had a game plan and the two oncologists agreed to consult together.

Honestly, this made us both feel much better, but we were so unprepared for all that happened next.

The clinical trial CJ was in was aggressive, chemotherapy dumped its poison into her body and the results were physically and mentally devastating. As I mentioned earlier, chemo can have a brutal effect on the body and mind, and it really put CJ through the wringer.

Going to the chemo lab for infusions was painful, physically and mentally. Patients are lined up in recliners in one large room and hooked to IVs pumping their bodies with poison. Some patients looked up when a new person came in, but mostly they didn't want to look. Or to be seen. It was horrible.

The family and friends who were with them tried to put a good face on things, but when they looked away their faces showed distress.

Most of the nurses in the chemo lab were caring and we soon learned which ones were the best with the needle, which ones would come by and check on things more often than others, and who to ask for crackers to kill the taste of chemo in CJ's mouth.

In the middle of her chemo treatments CJ got appendicitis. We took her to the emergency room and she laid in the treatment room for several hours before someone reached the oncologist.

It seems other departments, emergency included, are terrified of cancer patients. Maybe because they are afraid to do something that could affect the process of chemo and the fight against the cancer. Maybe because some of the drugs are hazardous materials. (There were some of CJ's pills that we were advised not to touch, even though she was ingesting them.) There are so many possible chemo drug combinations, I'm not sure even the oncologists know all of the possible interactions. So the emergency room staff seemed to take a "wait and see what the oncologist says" approach. When a chemo patient is in a life or death situation – like a near-ruptured appendix, "wait and see" is not an acceptable option.

I was kind of a banshee that night in the emergency room. CJ was out of it with pain, and once she got some pain meds on board, she couldn't speak for herself, much less run up and down the hall trying to raise a doctor. Not me! I hounded the doctors and nurses to DO SOMETHING. They finally did, and her swollen appendix was removed. I realized both how bad it could have been, and how seriously I needed to take my role as caregiver.

I made it my mission to understand details about her treatment, like food interactions, what would make her feel better at home, and so on. After some time (FOREVER it seemed then), she began to bounce back. It was a joy to see her recover from all this and to have some semblance of our lives back.

Of course, it doesn't end there – the effects of chemo can hang on in the body for years, not to mention the fear of cancer returning.

Complications from the ongoing medications and the ever-changing presence of cancer in her body still keep us on our toes. She is holding her own now, but those were some very, very scary times.

The crash

That first year or so, when CJ was undergoing chemo and recovering from it all, I was in fix-it mode. I was active and doing something, which felt good. As long as I was moving I could keep from thinking about what might happen. As long as I was researching on the computer, talking to others in support groups online, or actively giving care, I had energy and felt "good."

Bullshit. I was numb.

I would have crying jags in the shower. I'd jump in the car and drive around for hours aimlessly with no idea of where I was going, just moving, moving, moving. Whatever it took to keep going.

Eventually exhaustion and depression caught up with me. As CJ began to return to her capable self, the pressure was off. In a way I lost my driving purpose, and I imploded. I was barely functioning, going through the motions. I started drinking heavily; mostly at night so I could stop my brain from running off with me. I wasn't sleeping, in a constant state of agitation, waiting for an invisible shoe to drop. I couldn't focus on work, and I was losing clients. Alcohol didn't work of course, it just made me more depressed and emotionally pretty hard to live with. I would pass out at night and then wake up at 3 AM like clockwork, feeling like crap, dehydrated, depressed, ashamed, and hungover.

I was so confused. Shouldn't I be happy? CJ was on the mend, we were together, and we'd been through hell and back. We were even starting to get back on our feet financially. But emotionally we were in shock. And we were scared that the cancer would come back and not go away this time. Every ache and pain was the cancer coming back. Every cold or tummy ache brought back memories of when she was so sick from the chemo.

I sought out a therapist. She listened to me dump two years of agony out on her couch and promptly prescribed drugs. I hate taking drugs. I'm super sensitive to them, they make me feel out of it and wonky, which makes me anxious and depressed. I hated the idea of building up a certain level in my system for the long term, and feared becoming a zombie. There had to be something else I could do.

In the late '80s I was living in Oregon and working as a restaurant chef. I'd learned to meditate and practiced Tai Chi to help relax after late nights at work. I decided to pick up some favorite books. Pema Chödrön's "The Places That Scare You" and "When Things Fall Apart" gave me new perspective.

Pema Chödrön is the first American woman to become an ordained Buddhist nun. Her books address the emotional traumas of life and how to work through them, rather than hide from them. My personal favorite book for people who want to absorb key principles of Buddhist philosophy written in a way that suits our busy lives? **The Pocket Pema Chödrön** - chock full of easily digestible doses of wisdom!

In my research, I discovered how mindfulness was helping with depression, reducing stress, and how Mindfulness Based Stress Reduction (MBSR) was changing lives.

MBSR is a program Dr. Jon Kabat-Zinn founded in 1979 that brings science, medicine, psychology and meditation together. Through practicing MBSR, participants learn how to use their innate resources and abilities to respond more effectively to stress, pain, and illness.

Quite a lot of research has been done on MBSR for depression, stress, and physical pain.

In fact, MBSR is so highly regarded by the medical community that it is offered in many hospitals, including UMASS Medical School and the MAYO Clinic, to patients with chronic pain, stress, and depression.

A typical MBSR course lasts eight weeks, depending on the set-up, and brings the science of mindfulness directly into practice.

I took an MBSR course and went on a retreat for my first formal training in meditation and mindfulness. I was deep in the Santa Cruz Mountains, disconnected entirely from the outside world. I loved it. The idea of focusing completely on learning was right up my alley. Also on the retreat were other caregivers, as well as some patients and aspiring teachers. I had found my tribe.

MBSR turned my approach to self-care on its head. It made me realize I had a choice, even in the most frenetically paced days, to BREATHE, to be present, to slow down my knee-jerk reactions and respond more thoughtfully to situations. I stopped absorbing all the stress and let it wash through me, instead of absorbing it or reflecting it on others.

This didn't happen overnight, but pretty darn quickly I realized that I was less reactive, more capable of bouncing back from catastrophe.

For the first time I could see the knots I was twisting myself into and how to unravel the core of my anxiety and depression, finding a source of inner peace and resolve I didn't know I had.

I wanted more. I dove into learning everything I could about mindfulness and emotional intelligence. I attended the Wisdom 2.0 conference, a gathering of people from science, technology, and mindfulness in a variety of forms aimed at sharing wisdom and thought leadership in a community setting.

In a relatively short amount of time I learned to manage my depression, and found joy in my life again. The frantic clawing to find a way out of my feelings faded away as I learned to be more aware of my body, my emotions, and those of others. I felt more in control of my path.

I took courses online with UCLA's Mindful Awareness Research Center (MARC), Leiden University's Mindfulness program, which teaches mindful awareness to reduce stress, improve attention, boost the immune system, temper emotional reactions to events in life, and promote a general sense of health and well-being.

I learned new practices from Jack Kornfield, Tara Brach and Kristin Neff on compassion, forgiveness and gratitude at Berkeley's Center for Greater Good.

I attended classes at Stanford's Center for Compassion and Altruism Research (CCARE), which is a secular program focused on promoting compassion and altruism in individuals and society.

At CCARE, one of my teachers was a Zen monk and a grief counselor. I learned so much from the stories he told us of bringing compassion to oneself, loved ones, nurses, doctors and everyone around us. I felt myself starting to feel stronger, more capable of coping with our situation.

In that class I spoke with a classmate who was an ordained priest. He was exhausted from serving his parishioners, absorbing their grief on top of his own. He taught me how compassion had incredible power to heal and how he began seeing grief as a teacher, rather than a foe.

In 2016, I enrolled in the Search Inside Yourself Leadership Institute's training program (SIYLI). This program – founded at Google by Chade Meng-Tan – brings mindfulness, neuroscience, emotional intelligence and leadership training together to help people gain self-awareness and to focus, manage stress and improve resilience.

In addition, as I always do when I want to learn something, I read or listened to every book I could get my hands on.

I learned quite a bit about neuroscience in these classes, particularly that there are chemical reactions going on in our bodies and brains that I was not aware of. Understanding how the brain works, what happens when we are stressed, and why our stress runs away with us are key lessons we can all benefit from.

That panic, the feelings of frenzy and exhaustion and stress are due to physiology, and my new nemesis, cortisol.

I'll get into this more later, but get this, right now. It's not all your fault you're feeling this way, and once you know the causes? You can direct your energies to more important things, like health and wellbeing!

After a lot of introspection, retreats and meditation, I was feeling stronger, and more like myself. The drinking reduced to casual drinks with friends or at dinner. When I felt myself going down the rabbit hole again, I used my new tools to respond with more kindness toward myself and make better choices. It was like a door had opened to a room where I knew I could find peace and comfort.

Obviously, the ongoing issues of care and frequent moments of crisis are still here. But I am so much better prepared to respond to them without spiraling into frantic panic than I was at the beginning of all of this. Well, most of the time anyway -- I still have my moments of panic and depression, but I now know that recognizing and allowing these feelings to be present gives me the ability to deal with them more mindfully. I can work through them instead of stuffing the feelings and hoping they go away.

Living with vicarious trauma

Like many caregivers, I had gone into caregiving with all my heart, totally unprepared, and I didn't leave any room or thought for anything else, including myself. After six months of caring for my loved one, physically and mentally I was wiped out.

Over time, I realized what I had been putting myself through and the damage it had done, and not just to me, but my family and friends. I learned about Vicarious Trauma, a state of constant tension and obsession with the story or trauma experienced by those we care for. Witnessing their pain, fear and suffering can have a significant impact on the caregiver (amateur or professional), and in some cases can result in a diagnosis of Post-Traumatic Stress Disorder (PTSD).

Chapter 2:

The Caregiver Crisis

*"There are only four kinds of people in the world.
Those who have been caregivers.
Those who are currently caregivers.
Those who will be caregivers, and those who will need a caregiver."*
- Rosalyn Carter

The more I talked to people in the months I was preparing this book, the more I realized that we all know someone who is a caregiver in some capacity, whether we know that about them or not. If you stop to look around you right now, it's quite likely that more than one person you see may be acting as a caregiver for a loved one. More than 65 million people care for a disabled, chronically ill, or aged friend or family member in any given year. These caregivers spend an average of 20 hours per week caring for their loved one. Some provide 40 hours or more of care per week. (From a study- Caregiving in the United States; National Alliance for Caregiving in collaboration with AARP; November 2009)

Three out of four family caregivers are working outside the home while providing care. Many have full-time jobs and children or parents living at home on top of their caregiving duties.

With the high cost of healthcare and the additional costs of bringing a professional into the home, few can afford to hire an agency or individual, and so they double up with a full-time job and taking care of their loved ones, and make the best of it. This often results in stress and depression, not to mention financial and health issues.

About half of working caregivers say increased expenses caused them to use up all or most of their savings. They often keep the fact they are taking care of loved ones a secret at work for fear of losing their position, promotions or responsibilities, or that their boss would be suspicious of any lateness or absenteeism.

Who are the family caregivers?

A National Alliance for Caregiving study found the typical family caregiver is a 49-year-old woman. She is married and employed, and one in three have children or grandchildren living with them.

Female family caregivers are two and a half times more likely than non-caregivers to live in poverty and five times more likely to depend on Social Security income. (National Institute of Aging and conducted by the University of Michigan, 1992-2004)

The median income for caregiving families with one person with a disability is almost 20 percent lower than non-caregiving families.

Well over half of working parents caring for a child with disabilities say caregiving responsibilities have negatively impacted their work performance.

Given the above, it's not surprising that more than half of family caregivers experience significant symptoms of depression. And 2 out of 5 of these caregivers meet the diagnostic criteria for major depression.

(Zarit, S. (2006). Assessment of Family Caregivers: A Research Perspective).

Caregivers I've come to know

Over the last year I've interviewed dozens of family caregivers in a variety of situations.

Some cared for terminally ill family members, young children with developmental issues, aging parents with Alzheimer's or dementia, family or friends diagnosed as bipolar, or with physical disabilities of many kinds. I wanted to get beyond my own experience, in order to use what I've learned to help caregivers reading this book survive their own situations better. You'll find the stories of the people I've met throughout the book, including references to their own coping strategies and insights.

All the people I interviewed experienced significant anxiety and stress at home as well as at work. Fitting with the profile mentioned above, 1 in 10 were male or transgender, while 9 in 10 were female and between the ages of 45 and 60. Many had been caring for loved ones for a long time and felt responsible for being a voice for the patient with medical staff, insurance companies, family and friends, and at work.

Almost all of them expressed feeling lonely or isolated, overwhelmed and frustrated about not having the tools they needed to handle it all.

Most felt ill-equipped to handle their role, yet they committed time, energy, and finances to care for a loved one or friend. Maybe it was from a sense of duty, love, compassion, guilt or because they felt no one else was capable of handling it.

Even though many had other family members who could have helped, most were the primary person responsible for care.

Several said that in retrospect they wished they would have encouraged others to help, but they felt they simply had to manage things themselves, especially in crisis situations. This damaged relationships with family, friends and at work, sometimes resulting in breakups or divorce and loss of income.

Many were diagnosed with depression, anxiety, and stress-related or physical illnesses. These issues were often left untreated. Even though half said they had sought professional help, they declined medication or even medical treatment so as not to detract from their ability to care for their loved ones.

Almost to an individual these caregivers felt initially unprepared to understand the situation they were facing. They found themselves taking crash courses in illnesses and treatment options, and dealing with doctors, nurses and the complexities of the medical and insurance systems, in order to advocate for the best possible care for their loved ones.

Those who had a good support system at home or within their community, and who had other family members or friends participating in managing care, were significantly less stressed and felt they still had some semblance of a life.

Chapter 3:
You Are Not Prepared For This

"I just wasn't prepared for it. It came totally out of left field for me and for my family too"
– Marcelino

Here's the thing. Most family members are almost completely unprepared for the role we take on. Professional caregivers are trained to meet the medical needs of patients, as well as given a modicum of training in crisis management and effective communication. Professionals have opportunities to consult with in-house therapists, social workers and psychologists and can call on experts in the field for help with treatment plans and support.

They also get to go home at the end of the day. I'm not saying they leave their work behind -- most professional caregivers are extremely dedicated to their patients, often to the detriment of their own health. This book is dedicated to family caregivers, with great respect and love for those who do these jobs day in and day out!

Life gets complicated – very complicated

Lynn, one of the people I interviewed, found herself taking care of her mother, who was initially in the hospital for a minor hernia repair. During surgery there were complications that resulted in a partial bowel resection (a surgery to remove a section of the small bowel). After the surgery she contracted Methicillin-Resistant Staphylococcus Aureus (MRSA), a staph bacterial infection (often called a superbug). MRSA is tough to treat because it's resistant to antibiotics and can easily be spread from person to person. According to the Centers for Disease Control, MRSA infects somewhere around 90,000 people each year, with 18,000 related deaths. Abdominal infections are particularly dangerous when MRSA is involved, with a mortality rate of more than 40 percent.

This nasty bug can live for long periods of time on surfaces and everyday objects, and is often contracted in health care facilities like hospitals and nursing homes. So hospitals have a strict protocol in place for patients with this infection, including protections for staff and visitors. These protections include procedures for handling patients and whatever patients touch; even their laundry is a concern.

A long drawn-out fight for Lynn's mom's life ensued. Lynn was there for her from the beginning and to the very end. She told her family she was the best person to be there for her mom in the hospital, because she "knew what was going on."

She also didn't want to risk anyone else in the family contracting the disease. She was meticulous about following the hospital protocol at all times.

Lynn took a leave of absence from her job and spent an average of 12-14 hours a day at the hospital managing her mother's care. She had no previous medical experience and was completely unprepared for the stress of being a caregiver.

Even though she felt her mom was getting excellent care, and she liked the medical team, small mistakes made her feel it wasn't safe to leave her mom alone.

The protocol for a patient with MRSA includes isolation and specific procedures that are time consuming for each person entering or leaving the room.

Gowning up, wearing gloves, mouth nose and eye protection, handling the patient, medical equipment and bodily fluids must be done carefully to prevent spreading the disease. Lynn sometimes saw cleaning staff, nurses, aides and visitors ignoring or shirking a bit on the rules. She felt she had to be vigilant, not just for her mom, but for other patients and herself.

In the meantime, her mom was frustrated, in pain, scared and anxious to get the heck out of there. She wasn't terribly patient with Lynn and sometimes lashed out at her daughter, misdirecting her frustration.

Lynn struggled with herself a lot in those days. She felt guilty for being angry with her Mom and the doctors and felt trapped in her situation. But she couldn't see a way out. She was committed, no matter what. She swallowed her anger and smiled, smiled, smiled until she thought her face would break. Never once did she snap at her mother, the family who came to visit less and less, or the medical team, whom she did not want to anger.

In the end, Lynn spent three months nursing her mother back to health. The toll it took on her and her family was considerable. Her husband felt neglected and shut out when he offered to help, and stuck with running the family in her absence. The kids felt shut out too. She and her husband have reconciled now, but it was touch-and-go for a while, it took quite a lot of therapy. Once her mom was out of the hospital Lynn had to go right back to work, in a new position at a lower pay rate. She resented having to start in a new position below her previous one.

Her mother recovered; she is fine and grateful for all that Lynn and the doctors did. She doesn't remember a lot though, and is sometimes confused about details of the whole thing. She makes it clear that she appreciates Lynn's dedication and says so often to her friends and family. But sometimes she says she doesn't know what the big deal was -- it all worked out fine, didn't it?

That doesn't take into account the toll Lynn's absence from home and work took on her and her family.

In retrospect, Lynn says she's now learned valuable skills to manage any future crisis -- including not taking it all on herself and allowing others to help. Next time, she says, she'll ask for help and allow others to be a part of the process.

Shutting out and shutting down

Like Lynn, many caregivers isolate ourselves from the rest of the world. We may think, "I don't have time for anything else," etc., etc. We may not want to trouble others with our burden. We may not want to disturb friends, family or co-workers by asking for help. We may be embarrassed to share our "mess" with others. We may feel protective of the privacy or desires of our loved ones. We don't want to bother the nurse or the doctor with questions or our own issues.

But hey, wait a minute. Did we ask all those other people what they thought? Or did we just make assumptions?

If we build our own bubble, then we can stew in it, building more and more self-created stressors and "what if" scenarios. We can exhaust ourselves with ruminations and develop the idea that we are the only ones who can handle the task.

That is not true. Take a look around you. Look for those people who have lifted you up in the past and let them know you are struggling. Your friends, family and the medical team most likely want to help, but is it possible you've shut them out? Look long and hard at this and ask yourself if you are pushing away support. Can you open the door just a tiny bit to let some help come in?

Learning from Lynn's experience

There is a lot to learn from Lynn's story, and several of the people I interviewed had similar experiences.

Friends and family may feel that you are super-human and you've got it all under control. Be a little vulnerable and let people who care about you know that you are struggling. They may be surprised, and so may you by their response. Reach out in person, or even with a simple phone call, or email to reach out and touch them. Offer them some simple ways they can support you. Start with a hug maybe?

Nurses, doctors, therapists, hospice and palliative care workers are people who have dedicated their lives to humanity. Open your heart to offer them gratitude and they will likely respond with kindness and caring. Remember that they too have a heavy burden. A dose of humanity can significantly brighten their day.

There are also just about as many online support groups for caregivers of people with specific illnesses as there are for the patients themselves. Do some searches. Read through the groups on the websites and you'll realize that others are having the same or similar issues as you are. Talk to people in these groups and support them. Answer questions. Offer ways you have found to deal with their problems. They will return the favor. When we realize that we are not, after all, alone and that others have similar issues, we can bring compassion and gratitude to the mix. This can considerably lessen the strain.

When we reach out to people to let them know we need a hand, we empower them by giving them an opportunity to lend support and have a positive influence on us and the situation. When we accept their help and listen to their advice (even if we don't act on all of it), we lift them up and, at the same time, our own burden is lighter.

On the flip-side of this, look around you and see what you can do for others. A friend who needs to talk about their issues at work. A nurse is having a bad day and just needs a smile. Simple small kindnesses can boost happiness in them and in us, lightening both our lives. The more we can do for others the more impact it has on all of us.

In talking to so many other people caring for their loved ones, the one thing I learned above all else is this: every situation is different. There is no perfect answer. We all react differently at different times.

Some give up everything, even moving across the globe to care for a family member.

Some go into all out fix-it mode and try to hold the moon by themselves.

Some delegate care to a professional in their home and attempt to live a comparatively normal life.

Some go into overload and simply shut down.

Others walk away -- in fear, in grief, in guilt.

And everything in between.

It's not about how much they care for the person, love them or want to help. Many caregivers who passed on care to someone else told me they simply didn't have the tools to manage the demands on them in time, as well as mentally and physically.

In some cases, one family member tried to do it all, then transferred all the responsibility to another family member to try to "handle it."

Some felt they could deal with what had to be done, but over time were so overwhelmed they were hospitalized themselves.

In many of the stories I heard, the primary caregiver made a conscious choice to take on the role of managing the medical situation. This meant learning about treatment options, diagnosis, negotiating with the medical team to advocate for the best possible care. After they took on this role, the rest of the family generally deferred to them on decisions, and they immediately, or over time, became the sole caregivers.

Some families were torn apart by this, with siblings feeling disconnected, ignored or guilty about not being there for their loved ones.

It seems most families designate one person as the "doer", you know, the one who gets things done. Other family members may resent or feel guilty about that (even though they let it happen), which adds more to the caregiver's and the patient's stress.

Then, in our rush to do, do, do, caregivers run headlong into doing without taking into consideration the bigger picture. It's not always in the best interest of the patient, the caregiver, or anyone else involved to be running full-tilt without a break in sight.

Even as sole caregivers, it's a very rare situation that we can't find a moment to care for ourselves.

We need to find respite, if only for a moment.

Check in with yourself. How does your body feel, right this moment? Is there tension? Tiredness? Are you caught in a loop of "what if"?

It's time to take a break.

Forgetting to breathe

You wouldn't believe how many people told me they would be sitting in the hospital and realize they were holding their breath. It's quite common when we are stressed to breathe shallowly, sort of choppy and irregular, or to hold our breaths. Lynn mentioned she found she sometimes had to stand up and walk around to get some air moving in her lungs, as though she was trapped under water when she was sitting in the hospital waiting room.

Here's a breathing practice you can do anywhere, anytime; it can increase your energy and blow away that brain fog you get when you're tired. It's even said to boost immune function. Remember to breathe from your belly and not your chest. Let your belly expand when you breathe in and contract slightly when you breathe out.

(Note: if you feel faint or dizzy, stop this practice. If you are pregnant or have a medical condition that affects your heart or lungs, consider consulting with a physician for approval.) This is powerful stuff!

4-7-8 Breathing exercise

Sit comfortably, with your spine straight. If in a chair, place your feet firmly on the floor.

Exhale completely through your mouth

Close your mouth and inhale through your nose for a count of 4.

Hold your breath for a count of 7.

Exhale all the air through your mouth slowly, to a count of 8. (If you are comfortable with it, allow the air to make a whooshing sound as you release.) Feel that release in your whole body.

That's it. One cycle is complete. Repeat the cycle 3-4 more times.

What happens when you breathe?

This slow breathing stimulates the vagus nerve, which functions to control our nervous system. Stimulating the vagus nerve can slow your heart rate, increase relaxation and reduce stress and anxiety.

The counting takes your focus off everything else and puts it just on the breath, shutting off your worried mind for a time.

Feeling the effects of the breathing and the activation of the vagus nerve helps settle your mind and your body down at once. It has many other therapeutic benefits and has been used in treating PTSD and to control blood glucose levels. Studies have shown that having higher vagal tone influences the release of oxytocin, also known as the "feel good" hormone.

Make it a daily practice to give yourself a break with 3-4 of these breaths and you'll see the difference.

Waiting, waiting

In general, most caregivers spend a lot of time waiting: for medications to take effect, for the doctor to come, in waiting room after waiting room, or at home. Naps are good, but if you're wide awake or have to pay attention in a few minutes, the waiting time is a great opportunity to recharge a bit.

Give yourself a few moments for yourself. Even in the thick of an emergency room visit, practice your breathing to stay calm. Not only does that calm, settled, energy benefit you – it affects the person you care for too.

Things always go more smoothly when we are calm and aware, don't they?

Try reading or listening to a favorite book to give you some "you time."

If you can leave for a few minutes, take a walk. Get out in the fresh air. If you can't get out, look out the window and find something pleasing to gaze upon.

Try some of the practices described throughout the book and on the website. You can read them on your mobile device too, so you'll never be without a way to practice. There are some meditations and recordings there as well.

Chapter 4:

What Stress Does to Our Heads and Bodies

"Taking good care of yourself means the people in your life receive the best of you rather than what is left of you." -

Remember Lynn's story about caring for her mom in the hospital? During that whole process Lynn's stress went through the roof. She stopped being able to sleep and became irritable with pretty much everything. Her relationship with her husband crumbled and they fought almost every night when she came home from the hospital. Lynn felt like there was a constant threat to her mom's life around every corner and she was constantly vigilant. Maybe a little too vigilant -- but she simply couldn't help herself.

Chronic stress can wear down the body, particularly the cardiovascular, immune, and gastrointestinal systems.

Remarkable things happen to our brains when we are stressed.

Back in the stone ages our ancestors needed stress to survive. Let's put you in their sandals for a moment.

You might be walking through the forest, hunting for food, when you hear a rustle in the bushes behind you. Your flight, fight, or freeze instinct kicks in. That could be a predator, looking for lunch! Every nerve in your body is alert, heart pumping. You break into a cold sweat, the hair on the back of your neck stands up, and your mind is racing to identify the threat. Without you realizing it, your brain goes into action.

In the space of time so short it's barely detectable, your amygdala processes the threat and sends a message to the hypothalamus, the command center for your body. The hypothalamus signals through the autonomic nervous system to the adrenal glands, pumping epinephrine (AKA adrenaline) through the bloodstream, so you will be ready to run if necessary.

Vital functions like digestion, your immune response, and critical thinking take a back seat to responding to the threat.

The epinephrine coursing through your veins causes your heart to pound faster, serving oxygen and blood to your muscles so you can run; your liver dumps sugar into your system to provide more energy. Your breathing rate increases and tiny airways in your lungs expand to increase oxygen flow.

Senses like sight and hearing sharpen.

Remember, all these things happen before you are even aware of them.

Next, the "HPA axis" kicks in. The Hypothalamus, Pituitary and Adrenal glands work together to keep the body revved up. If your brain continues to perceive a threat, the hypothalamus releases CRH which travels to the pituitary gland and triggers a release of ACTH. ACTH travels to the adrenal glands and triggers them to release cortisol (AKA the stress hormone).

If the stressor continues, the body repeats the cycle. If the threat passes, cortisol levels fall, but slowly.

This stress response is important to help us deal with stressful situations, but we don't spend a lot of time running from lions or tigers anymore, do we? Chronic low-level stress can keep the HPA axis activated, sort of like a car engine that idles too high all the time. If our engine stays revved up it can have some serious effects on the body.

That epinephrine surge, if it happens over and over, can cause damage to blood vessels and raise the risk of heart attacks and strokes.

In our stressful lives, including if we're taking care of loved ones, cortisol can continually be triggered and the cortisol levels in the body get too high.

Besides the fight or flight impulse, cortisol levels can also rise due to disruptions in our daily lives or sleep patterns.

Complications of high levels of cortisol can include osteoporosis, high blood pressure, type 2 diabetes, increased hunger, increased fat storage (weight gain), fatigue, lowered immune system function, brain cell death and heart failure. Scary stuff (oops, there goes my cortisol again!).

Rescue mode

We live through lots of stressful moments while taking care of our loved ones. There are easily identifiable times when we are going full blast in what might be called "rescue mode." Remember my story early on about running through the emergency room demanding someone take care of my partner with appendicitis? My amygdala kicked into fight, flight or freeze mode and that HPA axis began doing its job. This compelled me to MOVE and make things happen. It also helped motivate the emergency room doctor to act and proceed with a surgery whose delay could have produced devastating results.

When it was all over, and CJ was resting safely in her bed, I went out to the parking lot and walked around in circles, burning off adrenaline. I collapsed in the car, exhausted and in tears.

This sort of process happens a lot, according to the caregivers I met. The feeling of the adrenaline rush in emergencies help us get things done, and the exhaustion afterward is very real.

But what about the long-term stress? As mentioned, when epinephrine and cortisol levels stay high over extended periods of time, it can literally kill us.

We need to learn to counter this stress reaction, or at least manage it -- instead of letting it manage us!

Don't get me wrong, not all stress is bad. We still may need to jump out of the way of a speeding car for instance; but it's easy to get into a cycle of constant stress, which is good for no one, including the person we are taking care of. We must find a way to prioritize what we freak out over and let the little day to day annoyances go.

As least for me, letting minor annoyances pass by is easier said than done. I found that after the intensity of being a caregiver, I was hypersensitive for months. My amygdala was easier to trigger; the smallest thing might set me off. That rush of cortisol and the lethargy that followed it had become my new normal, and it took some time to train myself to stop, breathe, and recognize what was happening, and learn to respond to stressors mindfully.

I've said it before, and I'm saying it again. Your own care cannot be ignored. You do so at not only your own risk, but at the risk of those you love. We make mistakes when we are over-stressed, over-tired, or over-capacity.

I heard again and again from caregivers that they did not take care of themselves, refusing to take a break, or even to fill their own prescriptions -- because they needed to fill the prescriptions of their loved ones. They didn't go to the doctor. They stopped paying their own medical insurance. They didn't take care of their homes, their families, their pets, or even their cars.

Meghan's story

There was the case of Meghan, who was caring for her grandmother, at home with dementia. While taking out the garbage and walking down the back steps of her grandmother's house, Meghan fell and hurt her ankle. At first she thought it was just a sprain, so she took it upon herself to get a boot at the drug store and wear it for a while.

The pain was intense so she took over-the-counter medications and stayed off it as much as she could. Then one day her sister, a nurse, saw the boot and asked about it. Meghan took off the boot to show her swollen ankle to her sister. On seeing the bruising and swelling, the nurse decided to rush Meghan to the emergency room. She had a fractured ankle and in the end needed surgery to put pins in the bones.

She refused treatment, because she "didn't have time." Her sister had to force her to go by moving into her grandmother's home, so Meghan would feel it was okay to take the time to get the surgery done.

Meghan had the surgery and some needed downtime in the hospital. Her sister had shown love and compassion for them both. The two of them decided to share duties and both grew closer than before, with each other and with grandma.

This kind of self-neglect is common among caregivers and it does no one any good. Untreated illness is common, putting the caregiver *and* the person he or she is taking care of at risk.

This isn't totally the fault of the caregiver, it's engrained on our heads from childhood. When deep in the throes of a long illness or a short-term crisis, we believe we should put the needs of our loved ones first. Everything else can wait, right? But for how long?

Just how exhausted are you?

Meghan was so busy caring for her grandmother that she neglected herself. She was physically and mentally exhausted to the point that she simply didn't see herself anymore. She wasn't sleeping, and she found herself burying her stress in a tub of Ben and Jerry's ice cream every night.

Self-neglect like this hurts more than just the caregiver. When we are in this state we make mistakes that can dramatically affect the person we care for and others. It's a great thing her sister could see the state Meghan was in and take action to help both Meghan and her grandmother.

Sometimes, like Meghan, we just don't have a clue what shape we are in until someone points it out. It's a whole lot better to check in with ourselves on a regular basis - to take inventory, as it were.

A body scan meditation is a great way to do this.

Body scan meditations can take from a minute or two to 45 minutes or longer. Most MBSR teachers go for 20-30 minutes to get a real feeling of what's going on in our bodies. I suggest starting with something short, just to check in with how you're feeling on a regular basis, then using the longer ones when you've got more practice.

I'll give you the short version here and you can find a couple of longer versions on the website.

Two-minute body scan

Get comfortable. Sitting, laying down, or even standing. You can close your eyes, or leave them open and direct your gaze downward toward the floor, if you're more comfortable that way. The point is to focus inward for a few moments.

Take 1-2 deep slow breaths, counting in through your nose 1-2-3-4 and breathing out through your mouth 1-2-3-4-5-6-7-8.

Breathe normally as you do your scan. Try to notice areas where you hold your breath. In those places make an extra effort to take a deep breath as we did in the beginning. Counting in through your nose, 1-2-3-4, and breathing out through your mouth, 1-2-3-4-5-6-7-8. Then move on.

Begin to check in with your body, bringing your awareness to the top of your head. You might visualize warm light flowing slowly down through your body as you go.

Your head, face, neck, shoulders. Where do you feel tension?

You don't need to fix it, just notice.

Let the warm light flow down from your shoulders to the length of your arms to the tips of your fingers.

Take a breath and return to your shoulders. Now that warm light flows down through your torso, your belly, your pelvis and through your legs to the tips of your toes.

If you run into tension, simply notice it and breathe.

Breathing

Throughout this book I'm going to suggest various ways to breathe. Take a breath before you answer someone to give yourself time to come fully into the moment. One breath is all it takes to allow your brain to stop, notice, and then respond in any situation.

Breathing is so taken for granted, it seems simple doesn't it? Breathing is something we do all day right? Yeah. Think about the last time you were stressed out. Take your mind back to that moment and really feel it in your body.

One of the symptoms of stress is to breathe more shallowly, or on the opposite end of the spectrum, more rapidly. Either way, we're not filling our lungs properly with oxygen.

Did you know that a large proportion of panic attacks are accompanied by over-breathing (hyperventilation)? When you hyperventilate your body gets too much oxygen and not enough carbon dioxide. You may feel light-headed or dizzy; it can even make a panic attack more intense. You may even feel shortness of breath, as if you're not getting enough oxygen -- when in fact you have too much!

Changing your breathing pattern can reduce anxiety and re-oxygenate your body. This technique, known as 7/11 breathing, is a powerful way to settle down anxiety, reduce the intensity of a panic attack, and shut down the hyperventilation.

7/11 breathing practice

Notice your breathing. Try to sit down and close your eyes. Just feel the breath going in and out. Now breathe in to a count of 7, pause briefly, then breathe out to a count of 11.

Don't feel like you have to make this take so long you're bursting. The important part here is that the out breath is longer and slowly releases. Breathe from your belly, not by puffing out your chest. You might rest your hand on your belly and feel it rise and fall.

Count to yourself and repeat the 7/11 breathing exercise four or five times, or until you feel calm.

Doing this practice regularly can reduce the number of panic attacks and anxiety in your life. Over time, you can see the panic attack when it starts and practice your breathing before it gets to a full blown state.

Taking care of your body

As we've already seen, caregivers are often so busy *giving care* that they forget to *take care* of themselves. This really matters. We cannot take proper care of others if we neglect ourselves. Mistakes happen. Important things get forgotten. Feeling guilty yet? GOOD. Take care of yourself!

Eat

As mentioned earlier, stress causes cortisol levels to increase and that makes us hungry. In Meghan's case, she craved Ben and Jerry's. I personally find stress makes me hungry for particularly bad food. Crispy, salty and or sweet for the win! No, the lose, actually.

Taking a mindful approach to eating can help stave off stuffing random junk food or even your favorite comfort foods in your mouth without realizing it.

Mindful eating is all about awareness.

When we become aware that we are craving nachos we can take a split second to be curious. Are we really hungry or are we just looking for empty satisfaction?

Yes, it's easier to eat takeout or live on a diet of Cheetos and Coca Cola, but not only is it not good for you, it's making you stupid! Really. Diet has a big impact on cognitive function, including dementia and lowered brain volume. Yes, your brain can actually shrink as an effect from high sugar intake combined with low intake of Omega 3 fatty acids.

High calorie, heavily-processed and high sugar diets are also directly related to diabetes, dementia, cancer and heart disease. You've got to take care of yourself, both for yourself and for those you care for.

In MBSR classes there's this lesson about mindful eating I'll never forget. You take one raisin and before you eat it you take time to look at it, recognize the textures, the smell, the color. Then you take a tiny bite and taste it before chewing the whole thing for a full minute. The idea is to really appreciate the food. Where it comes from, how it was grown. Who picked it? Dried it? Packed it and delivered it to you to eat?

I get the idea here, but I'm not crazy about raisins at all. Maybe in raisin toast or a nice Waldorf salad. And really, who has time for this?

Anyway, the point of the lesson is to take the time to consciously appreciate the food we eat. It also helps keep us from over-eating and to actually put some thought into what we put in our bodies.

This I can get behind. Here are some ways to work mindful eating into your routine.

Make a ritual out of how and when you eat. Instead of wolfing down whatever to get on with your day, think about what you will eat in advance. Plan it. Look forward to that part of your day when everything stops, and just for a few moments you work on satisfying your hunger, appreciating the food and where it came from.

Eat a bit more slowly so you taste your food, savor the taste, appearance, texture and aroma.

Listen to your body and eat when you are really hungry, not just bored or frustrated, and stop eating just before you feel full.

If you allow your body to tell you what it really wants you may naturally eat healthier foods; just notice when your mind is telling you that you need nachos!

Your body needs to catch up to your brain. If you eat until you are full you'll be too full in a few minutes.

Create habits around how, when and with whom you eat. Eating can be social and it's quite likely you need a little social time isn't it? We tend to eat more slowly when we eat with someone.

All of this too much? Start small. Just 1-2 mindful bites at the beginning of a meal can make a difference in your overall well-being. Seems worth it, right?

Exercise

Our bodies really don't do well when we don't move them. If you have a regular exercise practice, do your best to keep it. If you simply can't, find ways to work stretching and walking into your daily routines. Give exercise some importance so you don't skip it.

Simply going for a short walk, stretching or moving your body can help to significantly lower the cortisol in your body built up from stress too, an added reason to get off your butt.

In her recovery, Meghan discovered gentle stretching and yoga not only helped her ankle heal, it helped her body and her mind recover from the trauma. Later, after she was well, she kept up the yoga as a stress reducer.

Sleep

Our sleep can be disrupted by stress, changes in routine, or exhaustion. Pretty much every person that I spoke to said they lost sleep either because of constant worry, or due to the disruption in their schedules. Running back and forth to the hospital and then having to take care of family or work when they got home was a big issue too.

Try to stick to a consistent sleep schedule. Avoid alcohol, caffeine, or heavy meals before bed. Put that cell phone down at least 30 minutes before you go to bed.

If you can't stop your mind from churning, try meditating for a minute or more before bed. The body scan meditations in this book can be a wonderful way to relax your entire body and drift off to sleep.

Chapter 5:

The Role of Compassion

"If you want others to be happy, practice compassion. If you want to be happy, practice compassion."
−Dalai Lama

I enrolled in the compassion cultivation course at Stanford because I was desperately craving a way to feel better about myself, and frustrated at the way my life was going. Aggravated with the reception we were getting at the hospital, I wanted to understand how to grow compassion in my heart when I was feeling so very, very angry at pretty much everyone.

I was searching for a way to get my head above water. Overwhelmed on so many levels. At times I had to leave class because the pain was so on the surface that some of the exploratory prompts from the teachers and the group exercises brought me to tears. I simply could not do it.

Over time I learned that this too was part of my learning journey. I was becoming more vulnerable and aware of my own feelings. I was also learning to protect myself by paying more attention to my feelings and my body. Looking at them from a new perspective changed my world.

Compassion fatigue

Darius was 23 when his mom, Tracey, was diagnosed with dementia. His brother, Jake, was 15.

At first Darius thought she'd just grown forgetful; she had trouble recalling names or where she left her glasses. She'd forget to pick Jake up at school.

Then Darius noticed that his mom was having difficulty working through everyday problems. She had difficulty remembering new information and she couldn't do the math to double her recipe for her famous banana crème cake for a family gathering.

Tracey went to her doctor for a regular checkup and the doctor suggested some tests. Her doctor found that her carotid arteries, the vessels that supply blood to the brain, were narrowing, probably due to her high cholesterol. Her brain wasn't getting as much blood flow as before and so her ability to process information was slowing down.

Darius moved home to take care of Tracey and Jake. He was working full time as a software developer, and fortunately could work at home most of the time. He took Jake to school every day and encouraged Tracey to start a gentle exercise program. He and his mom walked together every day and they both found joy in these times together.

As Tracey's condition got worse her frustration level increased. She didn't understand why she had to stop driving, and Darius had to explain almost daily what was happening to her. Darius needed to be constantly on the alert, watching for an outburst from Tracey, while at the same time helping Jake deal with his own issues. Darius got Jake into a support group, which seemed to help. The two of them crafted a plan to run the household and keep Tracey at home as long as they could.

It wasn't long before Darius began to have issues of his own. As his stress level rose, he started having anxiety attacks, and his blood pressure went through the roof.

He couldn't sleep, worried that Tracey would wake up in the night and do something. One night she had gotten up at 3 AM and started cooking pasta. She went back to bed with the pasta boiling on the stove. The water boiled away, and the smoke of the pasta burning to the bottom of the pot set off the smoke alarm. Darius was also pretty sure Jake was sneaking out of the house at night and feared he was hanging out with the wrong crowd.

After a year, the constant strain of caring for his mother and brother was just too much for Darius, and he wasn't taking care of himself.

Remember that vicarious trauma I mentioned earlier? Darius was feeling the pain of his mom's inability to deal with her situation as well as Jake's confusion and fear that he'd lose his mom.

At work, Darius was starting to make mistakes, and his boss put him on notice that he was in danger of losing his position.

All of it was just too much. Darius was emotionally and physically exhausted and he saw no way out. One day he just got up and walked away. He saw no other solution.

After a day of being away from the house, Darius' head got a little clearer. He knew he couldn't leave Tracey and Jake to fend for themselves, but he needed help too. He sought out the family pastor and the two of them came up with a plan.

After reaching out to family and friends, they found someone to care for Tracey a couple of hours a day. It was hard at first, but both Jake and Darius found support groups to help them deal with the stress of caregiving.

Like Darius, many caregivers find that when we deal with heartbreak and trauma day after day, it takes a toll on us. Especially if we don't see the potential for real change, progress or healing.

This ongoing stress can lead to something called compassion fatigue.

Some symptoms of compassion fatigue are: physical and mental exhaustion, inability to sleep, weight gain or weight loss, irritability and depression. There may also be disassociation, a feeling of "checking out," or inability to deal with day to day care, depersonalization toward the patient, feelings of inequity in the recipient/caregiver relationship or with friends and family who "could be doing more." Other symptoms might be feelings of unworthiness or self-contempt, self-harm, substance abuse, or neglect and suicidal thoughts.

These symptoms of compassion fatigue are sometimes seen by the patient, their friends or family as a decreased level of interest or reduced quality of care.

We start missing things, things that could potentially be serious for our loved ones or ourselves.

It may show up in the workplace as inattention to detail, distraction, job loss, and poor work performance, and have a negative impact on work relationships. There may be excessive absenteeism, churning (continually changing roles or jobs), friction between staff members, staff and management or staff and customers.

In the caregiver's home, compassion fatigue can lead to neglecting family responsibilities, social isolation, economic insecurity, and divorce.

If you think you are feeling compassion fatigue, it's quite likely that you are. So what to do? Start by recognizing that it exists; awareness is key to moving forward. With appropriate support and information, you can start down the path to a healthier, happier relationship with yourself and those you care for. You don't have to make a choice between caring for others and caring for yourself.

Becoming aware of what's driving you

For many, compassion fatigue is driven by past events that caused trauma or painful situations that are being re-lived over and over and showing up in our own behavior. You may need to speak with a qualified therapist to learn to recognize and deal with these issues.

Anger at the medical team, our family and friends or even the person we are taking care of is also common. Lashing out gives us some form of release -- with consequences that are usually negative.

We need to get that energy out somehow. Rather than attacking someone because we are stressed, try getting some exercise. Take a walk. Play racquetball. Take up yoga, Tai Chi, boxing, or maybe knitting? What are the things you can do to relieve some of that pent-up energy?

The stress response

Laura Cousino Klein, a researcher at UCLA, conducted a study on stress and discovered that one response to moderate stress was increased feelings of caring, compassion and cooperation among the subjects.

In short, Klein found that stress can activate a desire to care for and protect others. That in time, the desire to care for and protect offspring or our tribe, can also be a stress response, and both men and women become more caring, trusting, generous and willing to risk their own well-being to protect others.

This "social caregiving system" is regulated by oxytocin. When the system kicks in, we feel empathy and a connection and are more likely to trust; it even inhibits fear. We become braver in order to protect.

This is followed by the "reward system," which releases dopamine (the happy hormone): you feel optimistic and happy about your ability to perform something meaningful, even under pressure.

After this, the "attunement system" kicks in, enhancing intuition, perception and self-moderation. This allows us to understand the situation we are in and the best action to accomplish a task with the best impact.

This ties perfectly into what I learned in the CCARE training at the Center for Compassion and Altruism at Stanford: When we feel compassion, we share a sense of suffering with another person, and a desire to take action to relieve or reduce that suffering.

When a caregiver has compassion for another person they are able to recognize the suffering that person feels and feel a connection to that person. This creates feelings like caring, concern and affection as well as negative ones like distress, frustration, fear or sadness.

Family caregivers have particularly strong reasons for giving compassionate care. There are familial or tribal connections between the person being cared for and the caregiver. With that relationship in mind, caregivers typically do not see the person they are taking care of as responsible for their loved one's own suffering. As well, in a family caregiving situation, there has likely been a history of positive contact and a relative attachment which creates a perceived responsibility to care and nurture.

Self-compassion

Janine was a young, single mom with two rambunctious 5-year-old twin boys, Francis and Jonathan. One day, she took the boys down to the neighborhood park where they loved climbing on the jungle gym and the slides.

She settled in nearby on a warm, sunny bench with her knitting, as usual, while they clambered around in a game of chase. She kept an eye on the boys, but she also wanted to give them space to play without them feeling too hemmed in.

She didn't see Francis fall, she felt it in her bones. She heard a sharp sound and a dull thud.

Seconds later, she was on her knees next to his still body and Jonathan was beside her, crying and asking if Francis was going to be alright.

Janine doesn't remember much of the ride to the hospital, or the first few hours in the waiting room. It is still a blur to this day, more than 5 years later.

Her mother met her at the hospital and helped manage dealing with the doctors and Jonathan, who was distraught and blamed himself, even though it was not his fault. Janine knew she could trust her mom to do whatever needed to be done, and that was a good thing, because she was a mess. She kept saying over and over, "I wasn't watching, I told them to be careful, but I wasn't there when he needed me."

In the end, Francis had the wind knocked out of him and needed surgery on his fractured leg to repair the damage. The doctors thought he would have a long road to recovery but predicted he would be fine.

A few days later, when Francis was home again, Janine began spiraling down into depression. If only she'd been paying attention, she said, Francis would not have fallen!

Any parent would relate to her thoughts, and most would also recognize that accidents like this happen all the time when you have kids.

But Janine couldn't let it go.

A friend from yoga class, Katerina, came to visit and Janine repeated her anguish. She wailed, "I'm a horrible Mother. Francis never would have fallen if I was paying attention. What if he doesn't walk normally? He'll never forgive me!"

Katerina talked with her for some time and helped Janine see that her sense of guilt, though understandable, was unfounded. For his part, Francis was already bouncing back (as children do), playing board games with his brother and wondering when he could show his friends his cool cast!

We must be willing to see that we too are experiencing pain that we are struggling. It's important to pause, take in this fact, and allow ourselves to respond kindly to ourselves, without judgement.

Often those who are most compassionate toward others are especially hard on themselves, denying themselves the same compassion.

We may say things like: it's all my fault; I'm not smart enough, strong enough, good enough, etc., etc.

But it's vital to cut ourselves some slack and allow ourselves a little self-love and compassion.

We must be willing to see that we too are experiencing pain that we are struggling. Katerina helped Janine see herself a bit more clearly, allowing her to see through a different lens, if just for a moment.

When we have compassion for ourselves, we see all the wrinkles, warts and temper tantrums, while also combatting that nasty inner self talk, trying to keep us down.

Self-compassion is a powerful tool for us to heal if we allow it into our lives.

Self-compassion meditation

Note: When you first do this meditation, choose a memory when you were suffering -- nothing too dramatic though! You want to start small here, so make it something challenging, yet manageable for you.

Bring to mind that moment when your life was challenging and you were suffering.

See if you can really feel the emotions and the physical sensations in your body that this time brings up.

Now, say to yourself:

This hurts

It doesn't feel good at all

I don't like this

These are very human feelings. We all have them, and that's okay. Acknowledging these feelings helps us deal with these feelings, rather than sweeping them under the rug.

Now, take a breath, maybe even put your hand lightly over your heart. This can be quite comforting.

Say to yourself: May I be kind to myself

Visualize yourself in that painful moment and ask yourself: "What do I need to say to myself right now to show kindness?"

This might be a statement like:

I am a good person, with an honest heart

May I learn to accept myself, just as I am

May I find patience with myself and others

May I see that everything is going to be OK

Repeat these statements to yourself.

Try doing this exercise the next time you're feeling that self-judgement has the upper hand.

Take a breath, put your hand on your heart, and wish kindness and compassion for yourself.

"Once we are honest about our feelings, we can invite ourselves to consider alternative modes of viewing our pain and can see that releasing our grip on anger

and resentment can actually be an act of self-compassion."

A journaling exercise on self-compassion

Journaling is an excellent way to work through how we are feeling. Putting words on paper can be cathartic, and helps us to see what is really going on in our mind, right now. With this kind of exercise, you're not writing in order to be read by anyone; it's solely for your benefit.

Here's what you do.

Find a quiet place where you will be undisturbed.

Grab a couple of sheets of paper, a notebook or a journal.

Set a timer for 1-2 minutes.

When you start, don't worry about what you are going to say or how it sounds. Let the words flow freely and keep writing, even if all you have to say is, "I don't know what to write, I don't know what to write, I don't know what to write..." Write that, and as your mind relaxes, more will come to you.

Below are two example exercises to start with; each has a different style. See which works for you.

Treat yourself as a friend

Think of a time that a friend made a mistake or was really struggling. Write down what their issue was.

As your best self, write down what you would say to your friend.

Now think about the last time you were struggling, or made a mistake.

Write that down.

What did you say to yourself then? Write it down so you can draw it out of your head.

Sometimes it helps here to think of yourself as a third person, watching what is happening and taking notes.

What could you do differently to treat yourself as you would treat a good friend?

What would a really good friend say to make you feel better about that situation?

Now go back and read over what you said to your friend, what you said to yourself, and what a friend would say to you when you've made a mistake.

Do you see that your self-talk could be kinder, just as you would be toward a friend in a similar situation?

Your inner critic

Grab your piece of paper and draw a line vertically down the center.

On the left side, write down all of the things your inner critic says about you. Use a voice that is in second-person, as though someone is observing you.

Use the phrases below as examples for what you might say, but fit them to what YOUR inner critic has to say.

Let it out!

You suck at playing guitar

You're so aggressive

You can't do anything right!

Now, take a couple of deep, slow, breaths and on the right side of your paper, write responses to your inner critic in first person.

I am learning to play guitar

I am assertive, not aggressive

I do many things right, and I don't have to beat myself up for the things I have to learn to do better.

This process can be a lot harder than you might imagine. It's hard to stand up to our inner critic and have compassion for ourselves.

If we can be kind to ourselves we can guide ourselves away from self judgement and negativity bias. We can reduce the negativity and self-limiting beliefs that are hindering our ability to grow and develop.

When we practice self-compassion we can find that we are stronger and more confident, maybe because we trust ourselves more -- we've got our own backs.

Chapter 6:
You Can Build Resilience

"The strongest oak of the forest is not the one that is protected from the storm and hidden from the sun. It's the one that stands in the open where it is compelled to struggle for its existence against the winds and rains and the scorching sun."
- Napoleon Hill

Sandy was diagnosed with breast cancer five years ago. She went through chemo and radiation for a year and then a follow up treatment for two more years. After three years of fighting the cancer, doctors told her evidence of the disease was gone.

She had been through a tremendous ordeal and survived it. While it had been a terribly difficult time in her life, she was feeling great, and more than ready to get back to a normal life. She started working again and loved her new job as a graphic designer. Life was looking good!

Two years after receiving her clean bill of health, she began feeling short of breath and went to see her general physician. He did some tests and diagnosed Sandy with a mild case of asthma and prescribed an inhaler. A month later Sandy was back in his office with worse breathing symptoms than before and pain in her chest. She had a dry, deep cough that wouldn't go away.

The doctor ordered a chest x-ray and discovered her left lung was considerably distorted; only the top third of the lung was visible on the x-ray. The rest of the area was obscured. After review by the radiologist, Sandy was diagnosed with a pleural effusion. The pleura is a sac that encloses the lungs and there is usually a thin film of fluid present to allow the lungs to expand and contract easily without friction.

In Sandy's case, instead of a thin film of fluid there was 300 ml of fluid in the pleura, which was compressing the lung and causing her shortness of breath, pain, and coughing. The doctors drained the fluid and analyzed it to find the source of the problem, including tests for the presence of cancer.

Three in 10 women diagnosed with early stage breast cancer develop metastatic disease, and Sandy was one of them. Metastasis is when cancer cells break away from the place they first formed and travel through the body to form new tumors. In Sandy's case the breast cancer cells had moved to her pleura and were blocking the tiny drains that normally keep the fluid balance in the pleura. This caused the fluid to build up and compress her lung.

Once the fluid was drained, Sandy could breathe normally, but she was thrust back into the fight against cancer again. Her doctor ordered positron emission tomography (PET), a scan that uses a special dye with radioactive tracers in it to locate areas of high activity and can indicate the presence of cancer through bright areas where cancer cells are multiplying. Sandy had bright spots in her pleura and on one of her ribs.

The doctor prescribed chemotherapy, and at the same time recommended she get her affairs in order. He connected her to hospice to arrange for end of life care. He said he couldn't predict how long she had to live. It could be three months, or, if the chemo worked, it could be longer.

Sandy was in a tailspin. A single mother with a 16 year-old daughter, she had a lot of responsibility and so much to look forward to in her life. She wanted to see her daughter graduate from high school and maybe go to college or fall in love. She wanted to make sure her daughter was financially secure. Sandy was not going to give up.

Sandy started chemo, and over the next six months had more fluid removed from the pleura twice. This particular chemo was very tough on Sandy's digestive system; coupled with frequent anxiety attacks about her future, she was a mess. She was obsessed with the idea that every day could be her last, and this mentally paralyzed her. She had to quit her job again and found an agency that would let her work from home. It was only a few hours a week, but it was enough to keep the family afloat for a while.

Teresa, Sandy's best friend from college, moved in as a roommate, both to help with bills and to help Sandy and her daughter. Teresa supported her by working with Sandy to organize her affairs, including hiring a lawyer to put the house in a trust and write a will, and planning for a potential move to hospice and her funeral. Sandy wanted to be sure she took care of everything for her daughter, even though she had never told her how bad things were.

Teresa introduced Sandy to a local meditation center that had a great teacher. Together they learned about being present in the moment and gained some knowledge about dealing with trauma. It was a huge help to both of them to focus on what was going on right now instead of what *might* happen in the future.

When I met her, Sandy had lived six months longer than the doctor predicted. The chemo was working! Over the next six months, Sandy and Teresa worked together to reframe their perspective on Sandy's survival options. Sandy began to bounce back, encouraged by the success of the treatment and her new outlook on life.

Sandy feels stronger for having come this far and the anxiety attacks have lessened. They never went away, but as Teresa says, they all have adjusted to the "new normal."

Although she still has cancer cells in her body, Sandy is determined to live her life and see her daughter grow up. She's found new strength and resilience to keep fighting, and keep living. She told me that in retrospect she wasted a lot of energy panicking and it made her sicker. She's determined to take things as they come now, and she's ready for whatever comes next.

Life is going to hit the fan

Every single person in the world either has experienced or will experience terrible loss and hurdles to overcome at some point in our lives. These things can be terrifying and even emotionally or psychologically disabling.

The stress can make us more rigid and prone to injury and illness, and unable to deal with even the smallest obstacles. Something as tiny as not being able to loosen the cap on the jelly jar can send us over the edge.

It's easy to look at people who seem to handle stress with ease as super-heroes, isn't it? In fact, these people may have exactly the same difficulties in their own lives, but experience and practice have made it easier for them to cope.

The good news is that resilience can be learned. It takes practice and patience, but you can learn to roll with the punches instead of taking every single hit straight to your face!

In general, we've all developed some sort of coping method, going back to our childhood. It doesn't take us long to realize that we don't always have things our way, and usually after a few temper tantrums in our childhood we learn to accept this fact and manage our lives more skillfully.

Sometimes we just need a break -- time to cool off and reflect on a course of action. Other times we may lean on a loved one or a friend for compassion and support. Still other times we need to act immediately and get things done. Even then, it's best to pause and take even just one single breath before leaping into action, to give our brains time to process a skillful reaction to a stressful situation, instead of an impulsive one.

Of course, the problem may be that we've been dealing with an ongoing situation for days, months, years, or even decades. In order to continue to respond mindfully to these situations, we may need to look at our automatic responses and re-evaluate them.

Managing our emotional triggers

We encounter triggers throughout our days, and sometimes we respond to them more skillfully than at other times.

Examples include: a driver cuts us off in traffic; the neighbor's dog is barking; an off handed comment from a co-worker annoys us, perhaps because we feel a little vulnerable in our job situation.

When we're in a difficult conversation with our co-worker and we get triggered, we can shift our focus slightly away from her grumpy expression – which sets alarm bells off in our head – to feeling the weight of our feet on the floor, or to our breathing.

This allows our mind to settle down, refocus and not be distracted by our emotions in the moment.

We can adopt a gentle acceptance of our emotional response. Instead of fighting against the trigger, we can recognize it, and by doing so, minimize its hold on us.

This gives us space to be more skillful in the conversation, allowing the emotion to pass through us rather than fighting it.

This passing through of emotions has been called "meshing." Visualize your body as porous, like the mesh of a window screen.

When you feel triggered and strong emotions arise, feel them fully, notice them and then allow them to pass right on through your body, just like the wind through a screen.

Notice these feelings passing through and not sticking to you. See that you are not this emotion; you are more than that!

Knowing that we have the ability to experience all our emotions without having to amplify, suppress or even act on them is a very powerful skill indeed.

Of course this ability to focus our attention and manage our emotions doesn't happen overnight, but, with practice, we can gain these skills, and manage our lives more effectively.

Self-management allows us to handle our emotions, so that they facilitate rather than hinder our productivity.

We can also choose to consciously delay immediate gratification for a larger purpose: pursuing heartfelt goals, recovering when our emotional triggers get tripped, and leveraging our inner resources to respond rather than react. As a result, we move forward from a grounded and focused state of mind.

This doesn't mean we ignore our feelings.

Not at all.

It means that we see and feel those feelings, recognize the emotions and allow them to pass through us, rather than distract us.

We can learn to manage our emotions more skillfully and still experience their richness and value.

For example, fear is a totally justified emotion when we find ourselves in a crisis situation like a car accident. But in that moment, our priority is to get to safety and be sure that others are cared for as well. If the intensity of the fear emotion overwhelms us, things can go downhill fast.

At times like this, meshing is a helpful way to focus on what needs to be done now.

On the other hand, skillful management of our emotions can also be helpful in our work as well as our personal relationships.

When we are able to focus on what needs to be done in the present moment, we can be more efficient and are often looked at as someone people can trust in a crisis.

We've all known the person who runs through the office like their hair is on fire at every crisis. Who listens to them when it is really important?

We listen to the person we see as trustworthy and responsible, who can calmly give direction, and quite often that ability to stop, recognize what is going on and then respond mindfully is all it takes to make all the difference.

This ability also makes us more adaptable and resilient. Is there anxiety? Of course there is, but being able to recognize that emotion and regulate how we respond to it allows us to keep moving forward and make change faster and perhaps more creatively, because our fear does not own us.

We can slow down for a moment and see more clearly.

We can act consciously and avoid problems before they get bigger.

All of this simply takes practice. Start small with triggers that come up frequently. Like that driver who cuts you off in traffic, for example.

What are you going to do about it anyway? Why get all road-ragey when you could take the high road and wish them well on their way, even send them some loving kindness and make your day that much better for it?

Even those difficult conversations with our loved ones can be easier if we approach them mindfully.

Give this a try with small triggers and see what happens. I think you'll be surprised.

Building coping mechanisms

Let's say you're confronted with a negative situation, like criticism from your boss on a project you just finished. That darn amygdala can trigger fight or flight quickly, and you react by either running away from the issue, standing to fight (your boss is clearly wrong!), or getting defensive for your team or yourself (he's still wrong!). Or, you can choose to learn from it.

Take a breath or two to quiet your amygdala and listen with an open mind.

Nobody is immediately resilient in every situation, but people who bounce back quickly often keep the negative from overwhelming them by finding and focusing on the positive in the situation. For example, "I didn't see the car turning at the stoplight and they hit us." The upside might be, "The car has damage but no one was hurt. It could have been so much worse." This is a learned habit.

Like meditation, practicing the habit of finding the positive can dramatically enhance your ability to bounce back. It's true that if you're stressed already and have lost some of your resilience, it will be even harder to bounce back and the negative will seem MUCH BIGGER than any possible positive element. So we need to practice in moments of low stress in order to develop the abilities we will need to respond thoughtfully, as well as to find those positive aspects.

During a quiet time, when you are not stressed, take a look at how you typically cope. What mechanisms do you have for dealing with issues? This is a good journaling practice. Write down a list of situations and how you coped with them.

See the ones that stand out?

How can these coping mechanisms transfer to other situations? It's likely you'll see some crossover.

When you go through an experience where you know you could have done better, give yourself some time to replay it after the dust dies down. Think of how you could handle it more skillfully next time instead of blaming yourself for "failing again." We learn from failures.

Mornings

Every morning, when you wake up, you can choose how you will frame your day. Start with what you look forward to, or with a gratitude practice.

Yes, you may have a challenge ahead of you, but you don't need to let it stress you. Take a moment to notice what you have to be grateful for, even if it's that you are still here, this morning, to enjoy another day.

Build moments of resilience into your day. Small obstacles that you overcome. Take a moment to notice them, be grateful for having bounced back.

Do a mind-body activity in the morning, like a breathing exercise to help calm your body and put it in a restorative and positive state.

What is your daily stressor?

We all have something that tends to trigger a stress response. For me it is driving in Silicon Valley traffic. I have a tendency to talk to myself about how other people drive. "Seriously, people can be such IDIOTS!!!"

Seeing my outbursts and reactions for what they are -- silly and unproductive -- has been hugely helpful to me. Instead of screaming at the driver, I now (mostly) find the ability to laugh at the traffic, take a breath, back off and send that person some loving kindness.

I can't know why they behave the way they do. Maybe they are having a bad day and driving their kids to school is THEIR stressor. Maybe they are older, or impaired in some way, and drive with a slower reaction time than others. Maybe they are new drivers. Maybe they are deep in their own personal crises and not aware of how that is affecting them. A little compassion cannot hurt here. And laughter certainly helps.

Shift how you frame it

If you feel yourself getting stressed, you can help shift yourself by recognizing that you are getting wound up.

Even that -- noticing that stress is building -- can give you just the break you need to respond rather than react.

It's perfectly natural to ruminate on what is stressing you out, or to worry, but the act of noticing it, even laughing at how you're "winding myself up again," can break a chain of behaviors. It can allow us to regain control of our emotions, and accept the situation as it is.

If it's something that has already happened, we can't actually take it back, can we?

Use self-compassion to turn off that vicious circle of rumination.

Change what you're focusing on.

One trick that works for me, is taking that deep breath I'm always talking about. Over the years I've trained myself to settle, to focus on just that one deep breath, to feel it in my entire body. It stimulates the vagus nerve and helps me calm, and allows me to decide what's next. (Instead of running around like my hair is on fire.)

This could be any kind of centering trigger you build for yourself. Maybe it's breathing, yoga, a simple stretch, Qi Gong or just looking out the window, seeing the world outside or turning your attention to a treasured object on your desk, the thought of a loved one or a friend. You might even create an archive of moments in your life you treasure to look at when you are feeling discouraged. A sort of vison board for happiness.

All of these practices can help move you off the hamster wheel of rumination and give you a fresh opportunity to come back to your natural center, your happy place.

If you can stay in that calm state for a moment longer you increase the beneficial effects. You can increase your ability to handle stress, and reduce reactivity.

With practice, you can develop the ability to be more resilient and reach a calm state sooner than before.

This can raise your threshold of tolerance and build resilience to self-regulate more quickly.

The more we can feel that resilience in our bodies, the longer it will last, and the more quickly we can bounce back next time! As we build this coping response into a habit, it will become automatic.

We can create our own set of habits to build coping responses by recognizing repeated opportunities to feel good throughout our day. Try some of these ideas:

- Practicing loving kindness for some random person you see on the street
- Taking a breath to settle yourself throughout your day
- Remind yourself to check in with your body. How do you feel right now? Really experience it.
- Is the pain that was bugging you lessened or gone? If gone, take a moment to relish that pleasure.
- Enjoy that first sip of coffee or tea or a bite to eat

- Give yourself permission to fill yourself with happiness and enjoy it
- Create a toolkit of ways to reframe your experience. How can you craft a positive frame on what is happening right now?

The more opportunities we give ourselves to notice these tiny moments, the more of them we will be able to see. (They were there all along, we just weren't seeing them!) Be with these moments, even if for just a few seconds, and learn from them. Realizing that this is good for you can help you be kinder to yourself and others.

Chapter 7:

Allowing Others to Help

All of us need to begin to think in terms of our own inner strengths, our resilience and resourcefulness, our capacity to adapt and to rely upon ourselves and our families.
– Steven Pressfield

In the hospital or during extended care we may try to be the one who handles everything, but that is not realistic at all is it? An array of medical professionals are there to help, and they are almost always better prepared to handle the crisis than we are.

We have to make smart choices. We can create relationships with the medical team, our family and friends, and organizations that exist to support caregivers. Or we can try to do it all ourselves and run ourselves into the ground.

Trust me, I know this. So does almost every single person I spoke with in preparing this book. Some tried to do everything alone and lost friends and family connections because of it.

Look at why you want to do everything alone.

Trust issues?

Ego?

Really step back and take a look. Then be realistic about the toll going it alone will take on you, on your friends and family, on the medical teams who will be taking care of your loved one, and -- this is important! -- on the loved one for whom you are caring.

Can you really give your loved one the best possible support when you are exhausted and at your wits end? When you're not fully present? When you are not familiar with the medical options or next steps?

In this next section I'm going to talk about just a few of the professionals you may call on to support you and your loved one in this journey.

There are a host of professionals to deal with pretty much everything you encounter in a caregiving situation. I'm not saying you want to hand everything off to professionals and back away, but understanding that you are not alone can be very helpful.

Medical staff

I had a long conversation with Tanika, a Registered Nurse for more than 20 years. I told her my emergency room story. She said: "Yeah, you sound like a lot of family and friends who come into emergency. They are focused on only one thing, getting the patient they are there with the best possible care as fast as possible. They aren't thinking about all of the other patients in emergency, who are equally important to their friends and family."

She nailed it of course. I was solely focused on what I wanted, unaware of others who also needed treatment and of the hospital staff's time and needs.

Of course, we are often focused solely on what we need, in that moment, but a little compassion and respect for these professionals who give so much every single day is worth considering.

We have to take our blinders off and be present for what is going on around us, while also meeting our immediate need for help. Having compassion for what others are going through, from other patients to the emergency room staff, will actually make life easier for all of us.

When I spoke with Barnaby, he told me about how he reached out to the nurse caring for his mother, offering a new perspective to the nurse, and in the end making things more pleasant for everyone involved.

Barnaby knew his Mom was sometimes cantankerous and difficult. She had Alzheimer's and colon cancer and she'd been in the hospital many times over a three-year period.

Barnaby visited daily and tried to run interference for the nurses when he could. His mom would lash out at anyone, especially when she was in pain or embarrassed.

One day he came in to find Joan, a nurse, in tears. His mother had thrown a screaming fit again, and had to be sedated.

Barnaby talked to Joan for some time and he found her a compassionate and caring person. He knew she was struggling with how to take care of someone who was so angry most of the time.

The next day Barnaby saw Joan again. This time she was a little better and Barnaby asked if he could show her something.

"Mom hasn't always been like this," he said. He pulled out a few pictures of his mom in better times from his briefcase, and told her stories of the mom he remembered. How she took in anyone who came by the house. When Barnaby was a teenager it was his house that his friends wanted to visit. His mom was everyone's second mother. They all looked up to her and when one of his friends was down on his luck at the age of 35, Barnaby's mom had let him live in a room over the garage for a year until he got on his feet.

After their conversation Joan had more compassion for Barnaby's mom. She'd stop in and chat with her when she had a break, and in a few weeks Barnaby's mom was a little less combative. She didn't feel so abandoned, and even when she didn't know exactly who Joan was, due to the Alzheimer's, she still felt warmly toward the nurse, and trusted her.

A few months later, when Barnaby's mom passed away, Joan and some of the other nurses attended her funeral.

Barnaby had shown Joan that he understood how difficult it was to work with his mother, and he also humanized his mom in Joan's eyes, giving her some insight into the woman his mother had been. This opened the door to empathy and compassion for all the nurses, and eased Barnaby's mom's distress at feeling alone.

It gave Barnaby a sense of ease and relief that his mom was being cared for by people who understood her a little better. He felt that he could leave and get some rest without worrying quite as much.

Palliative care

Palliative care is a specialized field dedicated to providing relief from the symptoms and stress of serious illness. These specialists are there to improve the quality of life for the patient and the family and are a supplement to the patient's regular medical team. Palliative care is not just for terminal illness, and can be useful at any stage of an illness, right from the diagnosis and through treatment.

Talk to the palliative care team about treatment options and choices as well as your goals and those of your loved one and family. Palliative care specialists can act as an intermediary between the patient, family and medical team, to ensure that everyone completely understands the options for treatment as well as the hopes and possibilities for quality of life.

The Palliative care team can help smooth the way for conversations with doctors and specialists caring for your loved one as well as help you and the family deal with emotional, social and coping issues, providing counseling and family meetings to keep everyone informed.

Hospice

The very word, "hospice," makes me queasy. My stomach churns at the thought of the love of my life going to hospice. That is totally unfair, but here's why I feel this way; after an extended struggle with congestive heart failure, my mother moved into hospice and died within a short time there. I was out of state, and by the time I could get there she had passed away. I was guilt-stricken because I knew she had gone into hospice and I didn't move fast enough to be there.

Later, my sisters told me that the nurses were unfailingly kind and in her last days they made mom as comfortable as possible. The care they gave her was compassionate and considerate of her needs and of those of the family. The hospice staff offered care for my mom, but also friends and family were supported in their grief.

My assumption that hospice is where people go to die is not true anymore. While the focus of hospice is to provide care for people with terminal illnesses that care can take place before death is imminent.

Similar to palliative care, hospice can provide services to patient and family months before the patient passes. Hospice can provide medicine, physical comfort, and emotional and spiritual support to those we love.

Visiting home care

There are many service organizations that provide temporary, part-time or full-time home care. This is a great way to keep your loved one at home and know that they are cared for when you have to be away. Some of the people I spoke with had drop-in home care nurses who checked in on the patient; others had part-time visits to cover them while they were at work. I heard many stories full of gratitude for the service of these dedicated professionals, and one or two stories of nurses who disappeared or weren't qualified. Ask around for good referrals and get references.

Psychological support

Family counselors and social workers within the hospital may be available for the family as well as the patient. Take advantage of their services and work through feelings that come up while taking care of your loved one. This is not an easy task for most of us, but you owe it to yourself, your family and your friends to take care of yourself!

Family and friends

Ruth's father was in the hospital with a serious heart issue on the other side of the country. Her sister, Jeanne, lived closer, but was an obstetrician with a busy practice. She felt she couldn't leave work to care for her dad. So Ruth said goodbye to her husband and three children and traveled 3,000 miles to move into her Dad's apartment.

Every day she would call home and talk to her family. She would call her sister and give her updates on her Dad's condition, treatment plans and anything she learned from the medical team.

Ruth was not a medical professional, but felt the doctors were doing a good job overall. Jeanne often had questions that Ruth couldn't answer and sent her back to talk to the doctors over and over again. Ruth was feeling useless, helpless and underappreciated for the sacrifices she was making. Jeanne felt Ruth wasn't stepping up and frustrated she couldn't be there to help. The two argued a lot.

After some time, their father passed away -- not through lack of care; he simply did not recover. Ruth and Jeanne? They never spoke to each other again.

Ruth had jumped in to help her father without a second thought. That was her nature, she was a natural caretaker, and had often cared for her younger sisters when she was a teenager while her parents worked. It seemed totally natural that she would take on this role.

Jeanne had no problem letting Ruth take the role, even though she was a medical professional. Besides, her practice was new and she couldn't afford to lose patients. But in the deep reaches of her heart, Jeanne felt she was overlooked and that she should have stepped in to a larger role in her father's care. At the same time, she didn't want to tell her big sister Ruth how she felt.

This kind of familial resentment is way too common. We don't talk to each other. Every family has that one person who serves as "the fixer." "Ask Frank," we say. "He'll know what to do." But did anybody ask Frank if he wanted this role? Probably not. It is assumed that Frank will step up; he always has before!

If you are the primary caregiver, it's a great idea to check in with the family frequently. Give them updates on the condition of the person being cared for. Give people opportunities to help in some way. We can't all drop everything, but by delegating certain tasks, you can allow others to be involved in a way that works for everyone.

Active listening

If you want to communicate effectively, start with listening. There is a practice called active listening that works very well when talking to your loved one, family, friends and the medical staff. The idea is to listen in order to really hear what the other person is saying. We tend to gloss over what people say, or to finish the thought for them. Try this practice and you may be surprised at what you hear when you really listen, without judgement.

Try the following exercise with someone you are comfortable with, to at least to familiarize yourself with the concept.

When I teach active listening one person speaks without interruption for one minute. The other person agrees to simply listen, without judgement. Next, the other person reflects back what they have heard until the first person is satisfied they have been understood.

Then they switch roles and the second person speaks while the first one listens and reflects back.

When we practice active listening, it is absolutely crucial that we don't interrupt the other person. Just sit quietly and give the person your full attention. Without judgement or preparing your remarks.

Listening is a simple thing to do, but how often are we listening to someone and thinking about what we want to say next? Or planning dinner, waiting for them to finish, so we can speak? Looking at our devices or over their head at someone we really wanted to talk to?

We may not even think of this as not paying full attention, or being disrespectful, but it is.

To truly listen to someone and really hear what they have to say can be quite surprising! We often have in our heads that people think one thing, and they say quite something else.

We miss their brilliance, or their pain.

If we make the effort to actually listen to people and what they are saying, we give them the gift of attention and we give ourselves the gift of being fully present.

Active listening is a technique to build real understanding, rapport and trust with the person who's doing the talking. It's about showing that you actually give a damn about this person and what they are saying.

It's important here that you are really paying attention. Put down the devices. Turn off the TV. Be ready to just listen, without any qualification or analysis.

Look the person in the eye and let them know you're there for them.

Allow silence to happen. People need time to formulate thoughts, and jumping in with your own perspective keeps them from expressing theirs. Take a breath or even two before you interrupt them and maybe you won't have to. People often fill in the blanks in their thoughts if we let them.

When they are done speaking, reflect back to them using descriptions of emotions: "This seems important to you because... or I'm sensing you are frustrated, worried, excited, etc."

If you're not sure of every point, give them a summary of what you think you heard and ask if that is correct. "It sounds like ..."

If your mind wanders off to something else, or starts formulating answers, bring yourself back to the present, without judgement. Take a breath and center yourself. Over time you can build this skill, and it becomes first nature to be present.

Feel free to ask questions to clarify, but be respectful and give the other person time to answer. Be kind and curious. Remember, this is a *listening* exercise.

Listening can be an amazing tool in the workplace or at home with family. Children especially seem to actually glow when given the focused attention of an adult.

Putting people in boxes

Don't compare your journey to the journey of others. Only you know where the journey began and how very far you have come." -

Here's something we need to train ourselves to watch out for. Most of the time we are completely unaware of how we objectify others, reducing them to their roles or our perception of them, rather than opening our hearts and minds to see who that person really is.

ob·jec·ti·fi·ca·tion - - əbˌjektəfəˈkāSH(ə)n: "the action of degrading someone to the status of a mere object."

When we think of the word "objectification," we might think of the objectification of fashion models or athletes as sexual objects. That's the most lurid and oft-used example anyway.

The truth is, we tend to objectify people we see every day: the janitor, the window washer, the police officer, the waiter, the cashier, the doctor, the nurse -- even mindfulness coaches!

We think of them as what their job description is rather than thinking of them as human beings, and when we do that, we separate ourselves from those people. We see them as that object and we treat them differently. With a person doing a job, we judge how well they're doing that job, and not what kind of day they might be having, how they feel, or what their joys or their troubles may be.

We often objectify people for how they look, act, dress or express themselves.

We put people in neat little boxes so we don't have to think about the human being in that box. We feel free to pass judgement and get on with our days without a second thought.

When we are in and out of business places, institutions or hospitals a lot we can feel like cogs in a huge machine, a machine populated by objects doing a job. We must remind ourselves that each and every one of the people we encounter is a human being with the same needs and thoughts and desires as anyone else. They want to be seen as a person. To be cared about, to be loved, to have someone to love. To be happy and safe. To be without stress.

If we don't say hello with something as simple as a smile, a nod, or a good morning, how does that make them feel? How does it feel for them when this is repeated by hundreds or thousands of people per day at work? Even though they don't necessarily see or hear that we objectified them, they can feel it, they know it. It's usually quite obvious even if we try to hide it.

In some cases, these human beings hold our fates or the fates of our loved ones literally in their hands. Do we really want to treat them like mindless objects? Or do we want them to be human?

Now, here's the trick. If we stop putting people in boxes and allow ourselves to see them as human beings, they are more likely to see us as human beings as well. Taking people out of their boxes takes us out of our boxes too. Are we more vulnerable? Yes, absolutely we are. But we're also able to enjoy our lives more, and more likely to have other people enjoy our presence.

There's only one thing to do then, isn't there? Can you guess what it is?

That's right! Notice other people. Smile. Say hello, even ask them how their day is and really mean it. Stop and listen to the answer. Maybe even have a quick conversational exchange.

You know what happens when you do that? They smile back. They feel noticed and that feels good to them. That feeling shows up in you too, because it feels good to do something good for someone else -- even, or maybe especially, if you don't know them. It's a lovely little gratitude fest and both parties carry that forward to the next person.

In essence, this is a form of the loving kindness meditation, where we wish the other person to be happy, to be safe, to be at ease.

A professor in the department of psychology at the University of North Carolina at Chapel Hill, Barbara

Fredrickson, did a **field experiment on loving kindness** meditation. Half the group received instructions to do loving kindness meditation. Over time, experiencing daily positive emotions produced increased personal resources like mindfulness, social support, decreased symptoms of illness, reduced depression and a sense of purpose in life.

Barbara called this the "broaden and build theory of positive emotions." The concept being that because positive emotions arise in response to diffuse opportunities, rather than narrowly-focused threats, positive emotions momentarily broaden people's attention and thinking, enabling them to draw on higher-level connections and a wider-than-usual range of ideas.

In turn, these broadened outlooks often help people to discover and build consequential personal resources.

These resources can be cognitive, like the ability to mindfully attend to the present moment; psychological, like the ability to maintain a sense of mastery over environmental challenges; social, like the ability to give and receive emotional support; or physical, like the ability to ward off the common cold.

People with these resources are more likely to effectively meet life's challenges and take advantage of its opportunities, becoming more successful, healthy, and happy.

End result? A happier you who is more responsive to the moment and more resilient!

How's that for a reason to practice loving kindness?

Learn more about this powerful practice called loving kindness in the practices section of this book, or from the meditations provided on the website.

Chapter 8:

Put Mindful Awareness to Work for You

"Mindfulness is: Paying attention in a particular way: on purpose, in the present moment, and non-judgmentally"
– Jon Kabat-Zinn.

I am not a certified MBSR (Mindfulness Based Stress Reduction) coach, I'm not a psychologist or medical professional. I am simply sharing my personal journey and what I have learned from some amazing teachers, friends, patients and other caregivers.

I wrote this book because I wanted to share what transformed my relationship with myself and others and allowed me to be stronger than I thought was capable.

Going back to my mindfulness practice and digging in deeper literally saved me. It also likely saved my relationship with my partner, my family, and with several of my friends. I slowly started to be myself again, yet more grounded. Even in the tough times, I am able to find moments of happiness and strength. The more I practiced, the more I was able to find moments of peace, and then, in time, clarity and an understanding that I am in control of my own path. No matter what happens, I have better tools now than ever before.

In this section are a number of ways you can add mindfulness practices to your own life. I suggest you start with one or two things that resonate with you. Try them a few times and see how it makes you feel. This is how we can form good habits, little by little.

Simply being present, right here, right now, with whatever is going on can make a remarkable difference in our lives. When we pay attention, in the moment, we aren't freaking out about what happened in the past or what might happen in the future. We are dealing with right here, right now. There are times when the ability to drop into the moment and be present with whatever is going on can be beautiful and full of wonder. There are times it can save your life, or someone else's.

Walking down the street and out of the corner of your eye you may see a beautiful flower, a laughing child, a secret kiss. If we are in the moment, no matter how the rest of our day is going, these tiny moments of presence and joy are irreplaceable.

When we are in the midst of a crisis, being present can save us from injury, getting in the way, or missing a critical moment that could make a life or death difference.

When we are waiting for something to happen while taking care of our loved ones, we have an opportunity to refresh our energy, drop into being simply present and just BE. Nowhere to go, nothing to ponder, nothing to do, just be. It can be quite rejuvenating.

Create good habits

We can develop little rituals to help keep us present. Lena's story is an example of finding ways to take a few moments for ourselves and to allow ourselves to just be with one experience at a time.

Lena's father was in the hospital and critically ill. She moved across the country for a month to be there with him in his last days. Like me in my situation with CJ, she had little knowledge of the condition he had, and researched it and potential treatments as much as she could. She was in his room every day when the nurses came, kindly and firmly insisting that they follow each procedure correctly. She felt that if she wasn't there something could go wrong, and the fear of a mistake when she wasn't on watch was overwhelming.

Lena knew that she had to have something to ground her and keep her sane. The food in the cafeteria didn't fit her dietary needs but she found a local coffee shop nearby that had a gluten-free menu. Each day after morning rounds, she'd go get a cup of tea and a particular salad. Then she'd just sit there for 30 minutes or so, completely in the moment with her tea and her salad. Always the same, every day, for three weeks. It may seem boring to us, but to her it was regenerative. She'd go back to the hospital and settle in with a book or read to her dad if he was awake. She said it was her one moment of peace to prepare her for going back into the hospital.

Create your own refuge

Jim hated hospitals. He'd been hospitalized as a child, and at the age of 6, he'd seen his grandmother die in the hospital, on a respirator and so helpless. Hospital visits gave him panic attacks. But when his partner was hospitalized for surgery he forced himself to go. A lot of discipline kept him there, loving and caring on the outside and wanting to run, run, run on the inside. Randy, his partner, was pretty medicated at the time, and was often sleeping. This left Jim to his own thoughts of impending doom. He tried meditating, but with all that cortisol in his system he couldn't sit still, so as soon as the rounds were over he'd head for the door and walk the halls. Moving, moving, moving. He knew every nook and cranny of that hospital. Where he could jump outside and walk on the grass between the buildings. Where the nurses went to smoke. The nurses got to know him and would wave or say hi as he walked by and he would silently repeat the phrases he'd learned in a loving kindness meditation. "May they be safe, may they be happy, may they be free from stress."

Finally, he'd get the energy out and be able to go back to the hospital room feeling peaceful, and ready for the next thing, whatever it was.

Walking meditation

Walking can be a form of meditation. You don't have to sit still to meditate, and exercise helps the cortisol from your stress dissipate faster. For Jim, it gave him resilience, the ability to bounce back and do what he needed to do, without the stress he'd feel if he sat stiffly in a chair in the corner.

It's interesting to note that cortisol levels drop faster with physical activity. Jim's walk was helping him get rid of some of what was giving him that sense of urgency.

Is it true?

Remember Janine and how she freaked out about Francis' accident, blaming herself? When I catch myself diving into self-judgement, or judgement of others, I ask myself a question I learned from Byron Katie: "Is it true?" I had no idea the significance it would have for me, but the impact of an apparently simple question is huge.

We all harbor doubts or fears about the future, about our abilities, about the intentions of others. Sometimes we let those doubts carry us away from reality. We get wrapped up in them, obsess about what could happen or what someone else is thinking or doing. Whether they meant harm or simply acted unconsciously. We are sure of the worst.

When I feel that sense of impending doom hovering around I look it straight in the eye and ask myself, "Is it true?" Is this really going to be the end? Did they do that on purpose to be hurtful? Really? Do I know that for a fact? What facts do I know? Really know?

Going through this question and answer process helps me get in touch with runaway thoughts and see them as they really are. Getting distance from my thoughts gives me a much more real perspective. It allows me to give a little space to the judgement and think things through before I let my imagination run away with me.

Finding happiness when you think there is none

Nafessa's partner has Multiple Sclerosis. The constant battle with pain, neuropathy, and fatigue, and the roller coaster of trying new medications, were difficult for them both. Especially when there was a flare-up. There were times Nafessa couldn't even touch her partner without causing pain and this made it harder for them to feel connected. Nafessa's mother gave her a book by Rick Hanson called *Hardwiring Happiness: The New Brain Science of Contentment, Calm, and Confidence*.

When her mother handed her the book Nafessa burst into tears. How could she even consider trying to be happy when the love of her life was in agony? Her mom encouraged her to read it though, and slowly Hanson's message soaked in. She reduced the impact of the negative feelings she was having by following his lead.

When she started to feel sad about what was happening in her life, she'd sit with it for a bit and let herself feel the pain and sadness. She'd accept that pain and sadness for a few moments. Then she'd take a deep breath or two, and as she exhaled, she'd feel the negative feelings drain from her body. When she felt calmer and more grounded she was ready to replace those negative feelings with something positive. She'd pull a cherished moment of togetherness and love from her memory, and she'd appreciate how that felt, bathing in the feeling and letting it replace the negative ones.

This is what Hanson calls, "hardwiring happiness." Our brains learn from experience, and those experiences leave traces in our brains. Donald Hebb, a Canadian neuropsychologist, coined a phrase in 1949 that goes, "neurons that fire together wire together." He discovered that every feeling, thought and physical sensation fires thousands of neurons in our brain, forming a neural network. Each time we repeat that experience our brain learns to fire those neurons together again. Or more colloquially, our brain pays attention to what we rest our thoughts on the most, and we get what we focus on.

So shifting our thought patterns to replace negative with positive is a way to maintain a certain level of happiness no matter what happens in our lives. This gives us more resilience and inner resources we can call on when we need them.

Hanson's book goes into detail about how to enrich our lives with happiness, hardwire it into our consciousness even. Suffice it to say that finding the pleasant feelings and thoughts in our lives and bringing them to mind often can make a huge difference in how we deal with the negative issues that are bound to come up.

These feelings can come from something as simple as warm sun on your face, the giggling of a child, a beautiful flower or the smile of a loved one. Cherish these moments. Bask in them and absorb them into your heart and mind. Your mind is a bank of these moments, there for when you need them next time.

Throughout the book I've referred to mindfulness practices that can help you. You will find a few repeated in this section, along with others that will be useful to you.

Loving kindness

Remember the study from Barbara Fredrickson earlier in the book? She discovered how the practice of loving kindness could broaden people's attention and thinking, enabling them to draw on higher-level connections and open their minds to new ideas.

Loving kindness is a meditation practice that develops the mental habit of getting out of ourselves, and offering selfless love to others. It can be practiced anywhere in almost any situation. It can last a tenth of a second, a minute, or an hour. Whatever works for you.

When I lead this practice with a group, I start with familiar people, someone you can easily think of warmly. This could be a friend, a lover, or a child. Simply imagine their face if they are not at hand, and think to yourself:

May you be safe

May you be happy

May you be free from suffering

That's it, it's that simple. You can embellish this any way you want. You can wish them to be loved, to know kindness, to have more joy in their life, to have ease.

Next we go to someone we don't know. Think of the cashier at the grocery store, the barista, the janitor in your office building. Silently wish the same for them.

May you be safe

May you be happy

May you be free from suffering

I LOVE doing this one in the grocery store line or waiting for my coffee at the coffee shop. Instead of burying my face in my phone I glance around and then silently wish the same for them.

May you be safe

May you be happy

May you be free from suffering

It may seem silly at first, wishing such things for random strangers, but I find it delightful, and sometimes I sense a gentle glow in the room (probably in my head) and it feels good. I carry it around with me for a while, and that is indeed most welcome. The more often you do this simple practice, the better for you and for those you're thinking of. Weirdly, even though the wish is said only in my head, people around me seem happier, friendlier. Is it loving kindness or are people just better than we initially perceive them to be? Good question. I'll get back to you on that one!

When you've had a little practice with loving kindness for friends or family you can move on to bigger challenges. Think of someone you don't feel so good about. Maybe a difficult person at work, the guy who cut you off in traffic, someone you're not so warm and fuzzy about.

Wish the same for them, and FEEL it in your heart.

May you be safe

May you be happy

May you be free from suffering

Believe it or not, this can soften your heart toward this person. It helps you to acknowledge that this person too is human. That they may have had a bad day or some suffering in their life. We can't always know what's happening in someone else's life, and practicing loving kindness for this person too reduces the likelihood that we will keep them in the "asshole" box. It may be as simple as seeing that they too have feelings and the desire to be safe, to be loved, to be happy, to be free from suffering.

In addition, your attitude toward this person changes, and it can subtly impact the way they now feel and respond to you.

"Realizing that the other person is also just like me is the basis on which you can develop compassion, not only towards those around you but also towards your enemy. Normally, when we think about our enemy, we think about harming him. Instead, try to remember that the enemy is also a human being, just like me." – Dalai Lama

Just Like Me

This practice is a wonderful way to remind us that we all have the same basic desires and needs, no matter who we are.

It's great for that person in your life you just can't get along with. The co-worker who just, well, bugs you. The family member who is well meaning but hard to understand. The hospital staff who are working hard and often unrecognized.

This increases the understanding that all others are "just like me." This practice can also be done alone, by bringing to mind a friend, a colleague, a neutral person, or a difficult person. Or it can be done silently, when meeting someone new.

You can use any or all of these phrases, or any that seem more appropriate for the group.

First, become aware that there is a person in front of you. A fellow human being, just like you.

Now silently repeat these phrases.

- This person has a body and a mind, just like me.
- This person has feelings, emotions and thoughts, just like me.
- This person has experienced physical and emotional pain and suffering in his or her life, just like me.

- This person has at some point been sad, disappointed, angry, or hurt, just like me. (You can say these one at a time….)
- This person has felt unworthy or inadequate, just like me.
- This person worries and is frightened sometimes, just like me.
- This person has longed for friendship, just like me.
- This person is learning about life, just like me.
- This person wants to be caring and kind to others, just like me.
- This person wants to be content with what life has given, just like me.
- This person wishes to be free from pain and suffering, just like me.
- This person wishes to be safe and healthy, just like me.
- This person wishes to be happy, just like me.
- This person wishes to be loved, just like me.
- Now, allow some wishes for well-being to arise:
- I wish that this person has the strength, resources, and social support to navigate the difficulties in life with ease.

- I wish that this person be free from pain and suffering.
- I wish that this person be peaceful and happy.
- I wish that this person be loved.
- Because this person is a fellow human being, just like me.

Now, how do you feel about this person? I'm guessing your heart may have softened a bit?

Smile. Feel a little better?

A meditation to lower stress

When we are stressed at work, or in our daily lives, our mind can run wild, thoughts flying around from one scenario to another. It's hard to get anything done at all, isn't it?

Especially as the emotions and feelings that go with stress show up in our body.

To manage our wild mind and see things more clearly we can take just a moment to recognize what's going on.

This can settle our mind and help ground us.

It can help soften the impact of any challenges we are experiencing.

Here's a meditation can help you get back on track:

Find a place where you can sit comfortably for just three minutes without being disturbed. You may wish to go outside, or close the door to your office.

Turn off the distractions, the email, the ringer on your phone; they will be there when you get back.

This is your time to recharge.

Sit comfortably, in a posture that is relaxed, yet alert. Take a long inhale, hold it for a moment, and then slowly breathe out, feeling the stress exiting with your out breath.

Give yourself a moment to settle in. Just be.

Close your eyes, if you are comfortable with that, or sit with a slightly downward gaze to minimize distractions.

Turn your mind inward.

Leave your thoughts alone for right now, and look at your body.

What sensations do you feel most strongly?

Your body may be experiencing stress as a sense of heat, or tightness.

Maybe your heart is beating fast, your breathing too.

That's OK, just notice it and give that area of your body gentle, kind attention.

Maybe you're feeling some heat or tension in your body. Notice that, and feel the energy of it.

We all have our own particular area where stress expresses itself.

See where yours is and direct that gentle attention to it.

Give it a little space to just be.

Let the tension exist there, rather than trying to push it away. Just rest with it.

If the tension begins to relax, just let it. It will settle down when it's ready.

Of course your mind may still be bringing thoughts into your head. "What if...," and, "I should." Let them be there, without judgement, or following them.

Like clouds in the sky, let them pass by.

Our bodies do mirror the mind. When our minds are stressed out, so are our bodies.

Good thing for us that it works the other way too.

When we relax our bodies, we relax our minds.

Gently bring your attention back to your body.

If your heart is pumping, notice it and give it the opportunity to relax, slow down.

If your breathing is fast, allow it to be, without trying to force it to slow.

Just notice, allow and give it permission to quiet down and if there is tension, experience it and give it permission to relax.

Allow your experience to be, and give it a chance to pass through, simply. Observe, letting the thoughts that spring up pass too.

Even when the world is crazy and stress is overwhelming, this practice will allow you to easily drop into a quiet place and find peace within yourself.

Beginning to recognize the feelings of stress in your body early can help you to manage them much more easily, and even shorten the amount of time you let stress control you.

I hope this meditation is a resource for you when you feel stress in your body.

Practice it often and you may find you experience stress for shorter periods of time, because you'll feel it coming and can deal with it more skillfully.

4-7-8 Breathing exercise

Sit comfortably, with your spine straight. If in a chair, place your feet firmly on the floor.

Place the tip of your tongue against the roof of your mouth, just behind your teeth.

Exhale completely through your mouth

Close your mouth and inhale through your nose for a count of four.

Hold your breath for a count of seven.

Exhale all the air through your mouth slowly, to a count of eight. (If you are comfortable with it, allow the air to make a whooshing sound as you release.) Feel that release in your whole body.

That's it. One cycle is complete. Repeat the cycle three or four times.

Two-minute body scan

Get comfortable sitting, laying down, or even standing. You can close your eyes, or leave them open and direct your gaze downward toward the floor, if you're more comfortable that way. The point is to focus inward for a few moments.

Take one or two deep slow breaths. Counting in through your nose 1-2-3-4, and breathing out through your mouth, 1-2-3-4-5-6-7-8.

Breathe normally as you do your scan. Try to notice areas where you hold your breath. In those places make an extra effort to take a deep breath as we did in the beginning. Counting in through your nose, 1-2-3-4, and breathing out through your mouth, 1-2-3-4-5-6-7-8. Then move on.

Begin to check in with your body, bringing your awareness to the top of your head. You might visualize warm light flowing slowly down through your body as you go.

Your head, face, neck, shoulders. Where do you feel tension?

You don't need to fix it, just notice.

Let the warm light flow down from your shoulders along the length of your arms and to the tips of your fingers.

Take a breath and return to your shoulders. Now that warm light flows down through your torso, your belly, and your pelvis, through your legs and to the tips of your toes.

If you run into tension, simply notice it and breathe.

This awareness of our body through a body scan is immensely helpful, and it builds with practice. When we are aware of how we feel in our body we can manage them much more quickly. We can learn to feel stress coming on early, take a breath or two and see what we can do about it before it gets out of hand.

Want to learn more?

I'm sure you understand that this is just the tip of the iceberg. The practices above are an introduction to mindfulness and emotional intelligence training.

There is so much more to learn and I expand on these with more content in the resources section and on the website.

I hope you will take advantage of these tools and learn how to care for yourself, before, while and after caring for your loved one. I invite you to explore a little and find the right tools to suit you and your needs.

In addition, feel free to reach out to me any time. I truly want to help you find ways to use mindfulness and emotional intelligence to ease your path through taking care of your loved ones, and through life!

This book is complemented by a website. You can access it at:

The website is fully enabled for mobile devices, including video and audio recordings you can watch and listen to on the go.

On this site you'll also find links to resources for:

- Caregiver tools and support groups
- Support links for patients
- Information about emotional intelligence and mindfulness
- Meditation and mindfulness practices
- Links to some of the research mentioned in the book

I encourage you to jump on the website, view the resources there, and let me know how I can help you further. Above all, I wish you well on your journey through life.

May you be safe.

May you be happy.

May you live with ease.

May you have resilience for whatever happens.

Index

A

active listening 110, 111
adrenal glands 49
advocate 10, 29, 41
Alzheimer's . . . 4, 28, 104, 105
amygdala 49, 51, 52, 93
anxiety . 11, 20, 28, 29, 44, 57, 58, 68, 86, 87, 92
appendicitis 15, 51
attunement system 72
autonomic nervous system 49

B

Berkeley's Center for Greater Good 21
bipolar 4, 28
body scan meditation 55
Brach, Tara 21
breast cancer . . 3, 8, 9, 84, 85
breathe 42, 43, 44, 52, 56, 57, 58, 85, 136, 140
breathing . . 1, 43, 44, 45, 49, 55, 56, 57, 58, 84, 89, 95, 97, 136, 137, 139
Buddhist philosophy 18

C

cancer 3, 8, 9, 10, 11, 15, 16, 17, 59, 84, 85, 87, 104
cancer cells 10, 85, 87
caregiver 1, 2, 16, 23, 25, 26, 27, 35, 41, 42, 52, 54, 70, 72, 73, 110, 146

caregiving . . 1, 3, 4, 23, 26, 27, 69, 72, 73, 103, 166
Center for Compassion and Altruism Research (CCARE) 21
Chade Meng-Tan 21
chemical reactions 22
chemotherapy (chemo) . . 8, 9, 10, 11, 14, 15, 16, 17, 84, 86, 87
Chödrön, Pema 7, 18
cognitive function 59
colon cancer 104
compassion 1, 2, 9, 21, 29, 40, 53, 65, 66, 69, 70, 71, 72, 73, 75, 76, 77, 78, 80, 81, 89, 96, 97, 103, 104, 105, 106, 132
compassion fatigue 69, 70, 71
congestive heart failure . . 107
coping mechanisms . 1, 93, 94
cortisol . 22, 49, 50, 51, 52, 58, 61, 125, 126
counselor 21

D

dementia . . . 4, 28, 53, 59, 66
depression 3, 17, 18, 19, 20, 23, 26, 27, 29, 69, 74, 117
diet 11, 59
dopamine 72

E

emotional intelligence . .4, 20, 21, 140, 141, 147

143

emotional reactions 21
emotional traumas 18
epinephrine 49, 50, 51
exercise . 43, 58, 61, 67, 71, 77, 78, 95, 111, 113, 125, 138
exhaustion . . 17, 22, 51, 62, 69

F

familial resentment 110
family and friends . . 14, 23, 28, 69, 71, 102, 103, 147
family caregiver 27
fatigue . 50, 66, 69, 70, 71, 127
Fredrickson, Barbara . 117, 129

H

Hair loss 10
Hanson, Rick 127, 128, 129
hardwiring happiness 128
Hardwiring Happiness: The New Brain Science of Contentment, Calm, and Confidence 127
Hebb, Donald 128
home care 108
homeopathy 14
hospice 39, 85, 86, 107
HPA axis 49, 50, 51
hyperventilate 57

I

insomnia 17, 54, 68

J

journaling 78, 94, 148

K

Kabat-Zinn, Dr. Jon 19, 121
Kornfield, Jack 21

L

Laura Cousino Klein 71
listening 45, 110, 111, 112, 113
loving kindness 93, 96, 98, 116, 117, 118, 125, 129, 131, 132

M

MBSR (Mindfulness Based Stress Reduction) . . 18, 19, 55, 59, 122
meditate 5, 18, 125
meditation 3, 4, 5, 19, 22, 55, 76, 87, 94, 116, 117, 125, 130, 135, 138
meshing 90, 91
metastatic disease 85
mindful 93
Mindful Awareness Research Center (MARC) 20
mindfulness 1, 2, 3, 4, 18, 19, 20, 21, 114, 117, 122, 129, 140, 141, 147
minor hernia repair 34
MRSA (Methicillin-Resistant Staphylococcus Aureus) 34, 35, 36
Multiple Sclerosis 127

N

National Alliance for Caregiving 26, 27
Neff, Kristin 21
neuropathy 127
neuroscience 21, 22, 148

O

objectification 114
objectify 114, 115
Omega 3 fatty acids 59

online support groups ..39, 67
oxytocin 44, 72

P

palliative care ... 39, 106, 107
panic 22, 23
panic attack 57, 58
partial bowel resection ... 34
PET (positron emission tomography) scan 85
pleural effusion 84
PTSD (Post-Traumatic Stress Disorder) 23, 44

Q

Qi Gong 97

R

reconstruction 9, 12
resilience 2, 22, 87, 88, 94, 95, 98, 101, 126, 129, 142
reward system 72

S

Search Inside Yourself Leadership Institute (SIYLI) 21
self-care 3, 4, 19
self-compassion . 1, 78, 81, 97
Self-compassion meditation . 76
self-neglect 54
self-regulate 98
sleep 48, 50, 62, 68, 69
social caregiving system .. 72
social workers 34, 108
Stanford 21, 66, 72, 147
stress 4, 11, 18, 19, 20, 22, 26, 28, 29, 35, 42, 44, 48, 49, 50, 51, 52, 54, 57, 58, 61, 62, 68, 69, 71, 72, 88, 94, 95, 96, 98, 106, 115, 125, 126, 135, 136, 137, 138, 140
support group 67
symptoms . 11, 27, 57, 69, 70, 84, 106, 117

T

Tai Chi 3, 18, 71
therapist 18, 34, 39, 71
therapy 37
threshold of tolerance 98
triggers 49, 89, 91, 93

V

vagus nerve 44, 97
vicarious trauma 23, 68

W

walking 48, 53, 61

Y

yoga 61, 71, 75, 97

About the Author

Janet Fouts is a wife, step-mom, and caregiver, as well as a public speaker, best-selling author, podcaster, coach, and corporate trainer. She has worn many hats throughout her lifetime, including dog-catcher, horse trainer, and chef.

In 1996, she founded a dot-com startup and transformed it into the digital marketing agency Tatu Digital Media. As a marketer, Janet is well-respected in the field, including recognition as one of the Top 50 Marketing Influencers over 50 by **Brand Quarterly Magazine**, one of the Top 150 Influential Philanthropists and Social Entrepreneurs by Rise Global, and one of the

Top 100 Giving Influencers on Twitter by Give Local America.

Janet has been fortunate to follow her heart in her careers and life. Her transition from the frenzy and technical issues of social media marketing to coaching people with a mindful approach to emotional intelligence is aided by her training with the Search Inside Yourself Leadership Institute to teach mindfulness and emotional intelligence in the workplace. She's also studied at UCLA's Mindful Awareness Research Center in their Mindful Awareness Practices program, and at Stanford's Center for Compassion and Altruism Research and Education (CCARE). She coaches individuals and organizations on a finding their own strengths through self-awareness and mindfulness.

When she's not working, Janet can be found spending time with family and friends, cooking (or eating!), or riding her horse in the foothills of the Santa Cruz mountains.

Learn more about Janet and her work on her websites at or on one of several social media sites:

- http://facebook.com/nearlymindfulme

Journal

Recent studies in neuroscience have shown that when we write by hand (rather than on a keyboard) we use larger portions of our brain and writing by hand activates different neural pathways. It also slows us down, allowing for a more thoughtful approach to the topic at hand.

I'll be honest that at first I resisted, but after a week of daily journaling before rising I found myself better prepared for the day and it also helped me work through any thoughts that came up during the night.

The pages that follow are intended for free writing or journaling. Using the prompts at the top of the page, simply write without stopping until you fill two pages. Whatever comes into your mind is fine, no need to grammar check or overthink it. Just write until you fill the page.

People often tell me the first few prompts are difficult, but after that, they bought a journal! It can be revealing and helps you get to the root of many issues. It also gives your mind a way to relax and just flow.

Give it a try and let me know how it works for you!

With gratitude,

Janet

When Life Hits the Fan

The best thing I can do for myself right now is....

Janet Fouts

When I don't take care of myself I....

When Life Hits the Fan

There is not enough time in the day because I am....

Janet Fouts

Caregiving has given me....

When Life Hits the Fan

If I could change one thing today it would be....

When I feel triggered I will....

When Life Hits the Fan

I am grateful for....

I am at my very best when ....

I feel better about myself when I can ....

Janet Fouts

When I'm tired I ....

When Life Hits the Fan

In the last 24 hours I smiled because ....

Janet Fouts

My greatest asset is....

When Life Hits the Fan

I appreciate ____ because....

Even on a bad day _____ can lift my spirits because...

When Life Hits the Fan

Today is the day I am going to...

Janet Fouts

I want to____ because...

I am stronger than I thought I was and I see that because...

Janet Fouts

Since I began caregiving I have learned...

List 5 people who have been kind to you and how.

I am grateful for the people who made____...

When Life Hits the Fan

My intention for this week is to...

Janet Fouts

I never thought I would...

When Life Hits the Fan

I had no idea I was so good at...

Janet Fouts

I'm so proud of...

When Life Hits the Fan

Each time I see ____ they/it make me smile)...

Janet Fouts

Today I can...

When Life Hits the Fan

Today I will make time for something creative by...

Janet Fouts

I will pause for a breath before I...

When Life Hits the Fan

What matters most to me right now is...

When Life Hits the Fan

www.ingramcontent.com/pod-product-compliance
Lightning Source LLC
Chambersburg PA
CBHW032038290426
44110CB00012B/861